More than Music Lessons

More than Music Lessons

A Studio Teacher's Guide to Parents, Practicing, Projects, and Character

Merlin B. Thompson

ROWMAN & LITTLEFIELD
Lanham • Boulder • New York • London

Published by Rowman & Littlefield
An imprint of The Rowman & Littlefield Publishing Group, Inc.
4501 Forbes Boulevard, Suite 200, Lanham, Maryland 20706
www.rowman.com

6 Tinworth Street, London SE11 5AL, United Kingdom

Copyright © 2022 by The Rowman & Littlefield Publishing Group, Inc.

All rights reserved. No part of this book may be reproduced in any form or by any electronic or mechanical means, including information storage and retrieval systems, without written permission from the publisher, except by a reviewer who may quote passages in a review.

British Library Cataloguing in Publication Information Available

Library of Congress Cataloging-in-Publication Data Available
ISBN 978-1-5381-6403-7 (cloth : alk. paper)
ISBN 978-1-5381-6404-4 (pbk. : alk. paper)
ISBN 978-1-5381-6405-1 (electronic)

∞™ The paper used in this publication meets the minimum requirements of American National Standard for Information Sciences—Permanence of Paper for Printed Library Materials, ANSI/NISO Z39.48-1992.

Contents

Acknowledgments		ix
Introduction: Build On and Exercise		xi
1	Sharing the Journey	1
	Student-Centered Teaching	1
	Curriculum Models	3
	Teaching for Inclusion and Diversity	6
PART 1: PARENTS		**11**
2	Parents Make a Difference	13
	Family Home Life	14
	Music and Family Home Life	16
	Teachers and Family Home Life	18
	Independence and Ownership	19
3	In the Lesson	25
	Step In, Step Back, Let Go	25
	Diverse Family Needs	28
	Taking Homework Notes	29
4	Meaningful Conversations	33
	Parents and Questions	33
	Acceptable Tension	36

	Parents' Most Practical Resource	38
	Teachers Letting Go	40
	Opening Doors	42
	FAQs	42
PART 2: PRACTICING		**47**
5	Framework of Basic Human Needs	49
6	Practicing and Autonomy	53
	Assumptions about Autonomy	55
	Language and Gestures	56
	What about Mistakes?	59
	Protecting Students	60
	Homework Notes	62
	Teacher's Belief in Autonomy	63
	FAQs	64
7	Practicing and Fluency	69
	The Activity Itself	71
	Repetition	73
	Creativity and Challenges	76
	Review and Refinement	79
	Slow Practice	82
	Immediate and Evolving	84
	FAQs	84
8	Practicing and Purpose	89
	Musicianship and Artistry	91
	Beauty	93
	Caring for Music	95
	Vision of Life	96
	Real-Life Stories	98
	FAQs	99

9	Practicing and Relatedness	101
	Teachers and Students	102
	Unconditional Personal Connections	105
	The Power of Smiling	108
	Sense of Humor	110
	Caring Relationships	113
	FAQs	114
10	Practicing and Reflection	117
	Developing Awareness	119
	Questions	122
	Silence	124
	Follow-Up	126
	Student Report Cards	126
	Parent Check-Ins	128
	Teen Student Reviews	129
	FAQs	130
11	Practicing and Listening	133
	Listening 001: Internalize	134
	Listening 002: Inspire	135
	Listening 003: Share	136
	Further Thoughts	137

PART 3: PROJECTS — **139**

12	Non-performance Music Projects	141
	Background	141
	Project-Based Learning	143
	Teacher's Role	145
13	Giving Voice to Students	149
	Students' Everyday Musical Connections Projects	149
	Junior High Threshold	151

	Amplifying Student's Musical Persona	152
	FAQs	154
PART 4: CHARACTER		**157**
14	Imprinted from Birth	159
	My Gallery of Student Portraits	162
	Connecting with Life Skills	164
15	Character and Music Lessons	169
	Exercising Character	170
	Empathy Starters	172
	Talking about Soul	173
	Character Reflections	174
	More than Music	176
	FAQs	179
16	Finale: Our Shared Humanity	181

Appendix A: Challenges	185
Appendix B: Parent Letter and Teenager Letter	189
Appendix C: Everyday Music Connections Projects	193
Appendix D: Character Cards	201
Bibliography	203
Index	209
About the Author	211

Acknowledgments

There's something quite remarkable about how ideas develop. A quiet conversation sets off rumblings deep in the back of your mind. The look on a student's face triggers an awareness so vital that you can't imagine why you didn't see it sooner. While reading a book that a colleague suggested, a certain line makes you feel like you've uncovered the map to enlightenment. Wondrous and beyond explanation, it's as if ideas have a life of their own, a way of finding other ideas and coming together to make sense in new and revolutionary ways. How does it all work? What makes ideas percolate? What keeps an author going long enough to pull together ideas into a book?

Ultimately, what's kept me going through this remarkable idea escapade is the interest expressed by others regarding the writing of this book. Their timely inquiries, such as –"How is the book going?" and "When will it be finished?" have kept me moving forward. So this grand adventure in music teaching comes with humble acknowledgment, gratitude, and appreciation for those whose interest knowingly and unknowingly influenced the ideas contained within.

I am especially grateful to my partner, Alan Antioquia, whose passion for life and teaching, endless reservoir of patience, capacity for comprehending even the most obscure, ambiguous, and badly expressed thoughts, has made this adventure seem worthwhile.

I am immensely indebted to Michael Tan, acquisitions editor at Rowman & Littlefield, whose confidence and guidance propelled this book to the finish line. His insight and capacity to inspire creative rethinking is exceptional.

My deep appreciation goes to colleague and deep thinker Trish Baehr. She has an amazing eye for detail and the uncanny ability to shed light on well-hidden blind spots.

Thanks to Jane Thomas, a fellow writer always willing to read the short and long versions of the manuscript.

Thanks as well to my colleagues Lorrie Merrell, Shu-Yi Scott, Wan Tsai Chen, Connie Bell, Carey Hockett, and Karen Zalter. Their thoughtful questions and conversations helped with solidifying clear directions. Thank you all.

Gratitude goes to my students and their parents. Their honesty and purposefulness inspired me to reflect on what meaningful music studio teaching might look like.

Special thanks to Naira Sidi for her last-minute advice.

Finally, I'm grateful for the following journals: *American Music Teacher, American Suzuki Journal,* and *MTNA E-Journal*. It's amazing how ideas from articles I have written in journals would evolve and adjust, converse with other thoughts, and join the journey to create this book.

Introduction

Build On and Exercise

Learning to sing or play a musical instrument is a wonderful adventure that music teachers hope to influence, inspire, and inform. And there's a lot for teachers to accomplish during weekly music lessons: technique, reading notes, playing by ear, pop music, improvisation, scales, repertoire, theory, and the list goes on. So, it may come as a surprise that not one of these curriculum-based topics feature prominently in this book. *More than Music Lessons* shifts the focus away from established music curricula to something of equal importance—the personal and interpersonal dynamics of students' own musical life. This book demonstrates what can happen when music teachers take an interest in and have an ongoing appreciation for their students' home life, sense of self, musical interests, personal and world views, culture, and spiritual individuality. All these factors come into play as vibrant underpinnings for conversations and interactions in support of students' musical development. Weekly lessons provide ample opportunity for teachers to draw from and amplify the massive breadth of students' personal and musical realms.

More than Music Lessons gets right to the heart of the matter with its twenty-first-century instructional philosophy: that teachers build on and exercise what's already there. Tailored to meet the unique demands of today's culturally diverse population, this book breaks new ground, offering music teachers a comprehensive vision of music education and practical steps for bringing inclusive teaching to life. When teachers build on and exercise what's already there, they share the musical journey that belongs to students. Teachers are curious and attentive listeners. They excel as collaborators, using their knowledge to support their students. They create curricula that showcase music as a catalyst for personal expression and social change. Music isn't something students explore separately from everything else in their lives. Students' musical development thrives when teachers combine musical knowledge and expertise with the real-life dynamics of students' personal, interpersonal, and musical lives.

Teaching Tip

√ Build on and exercise what's already there.

1. Be curious.
2. Listen.
3. Collaborate.

In *More than Music Lessons*, readers will find a comprehensive exploration of a student-centered (person-focused) approach to teaching, which differs from a curriculum-based (content-based) instructional approach. This student-centered focus is deliberate, given the extensive curriculum-based resources already available in terms of methodology books, comprehensive theory and history programs, repertoire planning and interpretation, exam preparation, and efficient technical methods. This book has been developed in response to noticeable gaps created by the longstanding instructional emphasis on curriculum.

A book for personal and social change, *More than Music Lessons* is grounded in research yet enriched with imagination and creativity. It presents a picture of music education as socially relevant, inclusive, accessible, and culturally diverse. By recognizing how students, parents, and teachers want to be valued for who they are and what they do, music teachers may not only develop thriving music education settings, but also sow the seeds for meaningful personal and interpersonal explorations beyond the music studio. With a focus on building on and exercising what's already there, four themes—Parents, Practicing, Projects, and Character—provide a dynamic framework for *More than Music Lessons*.

Chapter 1 gets things underway with a twenty-first-century snapshot of student-centered teaching—the idea that rather than teaching *at* their students, teachers *share* their students' learning journey. Curriculum models also play an important role in student-centered teaching. Furthermore, this chapter examines the importance of teaching for inclusion and diversity.

Part 1 recognizes students' family home life as a potent synthesis of personalities, relationships, cultural values, and activities. Parents and children give family shape through their individual personalities and the relationships they have with each other. Music weaves like a resonant thread into the fabric of family home life. When teachers respect the diversity of students' family home life, they focus on acceptance, care, and inclusion rather than attempting to reconfigure students and parents into some kind of idealized musical configuration. They support real-life parents in raising independent children and facilitate evolving stages of parental involvement. Teachers build on and exercise the principles and beliefs, available resources, limitations, and opportunities that are already there. Topics include the acknowledgment that parents may encounter certain acceptable tensions with their child and the recognition that parent peers are their most practical resource.

Part 2 takes on the mammoth topic of practicing by exploring five human needs: autonomy, fluency, purpose, relatedness, and reflection. These needs play key roles in the infinite number of learning activities that make us feel secure, capable, vital, and socially integrated. Knowing about them explains a lot about practicing. Especially, that when practicing doesn't fulfill any of these needs, students may find it boring or worthless. Conversely, when practicing responds to these needs or combinations of them, students experience it as something that's essential to their own lives, character, and identity. Practicing fulfills a need that all individuals have to validate their sense of self. Part 2 also addresses an additional aspect related to practicing and learning to play a musical instrument—*listening*—our need to transform the sounds in our heads into the sounds we make in performance.

Part 3 explores how teachers can incorporate non-performance projects to highlight their students' private musical world, their own relation with music, and their own personal character. Following a project-based approach, teachers facilitate, collaborate, mentor, and guide students' exploration of their own everyday connections with music. Non-performance projects bring fresh energy to students' musical development by reinforcing their relationship with music and providing opportunity for students to demonstrate their disciplinary knowledge of music. The goal is to help students put together projects that genuinely amplify their musical persona.

Part 4 places the concept of "character" on center stage. Character pulls together notions of personal authenticity, calling, life force, soul, fate, and sense of self imprinted from the day of birth. Character is what nurses in birthing centers indentify in newborns from day one. It's what an eighty-year-old man refers to when he claims he's the same person as he was at age ten. Teachers get to know students' character both spontaneously and gradually over years of working together. Part 4 traces the etymological/historical roots of the term "character" and examines the practical connections with life skills. On a more creative side, Part 4 uses poetry, metaphor, and poetic prose to stimulate students' thought processes and musical explorations. The goal in weaving character through music-making is for students to gain greater awareness and experience with expressing their own authentic voice. This means teachers assist students in connecting their inner world of emotions, consciousness, and transcendence to their external world of words and physical actions. Musical exploration provides a safe space for students to work through the big and small decisions that inevitably impact how they view themselves and what they're going to do with life.

Music teachers, professionals, parents, and students interested in the rewarding process of learning to sing or play a musical instrument will find many music- and education-related topics to try out or adapt. Likewise private instructors, conservatory teachers, and college professors. Instructional examples and scenarios in this book were chosen to resonate with the diversity in students' age, ambitions, and cultural experiences that today's music teachers routinely encounter. Music teachers are encouraged to use the examples and scenarios as a launching pad for developing strategies appropriate to the specific demands of vocal and instrumental performance.

With its focus on the personal side of teaching, *More than Music Lessons* aims to help teachers in responding to the current societal push for more inclusive and humanistic interactions. The goal is to spark fresh thoughts and conversations about how teaching may influence students' overall musical and personal development. Teachers are encouraged to read this book at a leisurely pace that allows space for the book's ideas and questions/answers to take shape. With this in mind, readers will find various layers to *More than Music Lessons*. Included throughout are:

- Teaching Tips: more than fifty practical and inspirational tips for vocal and instrumental performance teachers.
- From MBT's Studio: pivotal experiences with students and parents that shaped my forty-year music teaching career.
- Your Thoughts: ongoing, reflective explorations to engage music teachers.
- Frequently Asked Questions: answers to questions that deserve thorough and thoughtful response.
- Substantial research from the fields of self-determination theory, humanistic psychology, and project-based learning.
- Comprehensive resources for a student-centered (person-focused) approach to music teaching.

Music teachers will discover many of the ideas expressed in *More than Music Lessons* may already be present in their teaching. Some may be fully formed. Others may feel like seeds only freshly sown. Still other ideas may seem like distant stars, intriguing but far away. How can music teachers make the most of these ideas? Two ways come to mind. The first is integration.

Simply choose one idea from this book and see what you can do to integrate it more intentionally in your teaching. Try it multiple times over the course of a week with as many different students as you can and see where it leads. Multiple exposures to any idea can be extremely beneficial in understanding its effective application. The second is conversation. Turn any of the ideas into a topic for discussion with colleagues, family members, or friends. Observe how your explanations and subsequent explorations may shed further light on the idea and its application beyond the music lesson. Talking about concepts helps to clarify and cement them in your mind. It's a sure way to find out what we really think about them.

My hope is that teachers will repeatedly return to read, question, and revisit *More than Music Lessons*. My purpose in pulling these ideas together is to inspire teachers to develop a thoughtful vision and practice of teaching. I hope the reflective experience of reading this book will inform the way teachers invigorate and inspire who their students are and what they do.

Build On and Exercise What's Already There

The instructional philosophy behind *More than Music Lessons* is a simple one: teachers build on and exercise what's already there.

1. What does this expression mean to you?
2. How do you think "building on and exercising what's already there" is currently evident in your own teaching?

Chapter 1

Sharing the Journey

What does it mean to be a music teacher in the twenty-first century? What words can be used to describe what teachers do? Ask any group of music teachers and you might expect to hear them describe their teaching in many different ways. They may mention words like "mentor," "demonstrate," "educate," "model," "empower," "facilitate," "guide," "instruct," "nurture." All excellent terms that remind us that teaching is more than what teachers know or pass on. Teaching is very much about students. It's about teachers sharing the journey of their students' learning.

For today's music teachers, sharing their students' learning journey entails drawing from the various nuances of student-centered teaching. This means teachers envision teaching as a partnership whereby they learn and work *with* students, in contrast to teaching *at* them. Somehow, teachers need to lead the way, walk alongside, get behind, and let go of students, which is an extraordinary undertaking by any means.

STUDENT-CENTERED TEACHING

Also known as learner-centered education, student-centered teaching has a long scholarly and curricular history in the field of education. This pedagogic approach emphasizes student participation, ownership, and autonomy as essential elements in effective educational processes. During the twentieth century, the development of student-centered teaching evolved under the influence of education theorists John Dewey, Lev Vygotsky, and Jean Piaget, as well as education pioneer Maria Montessori, who advocated for educational processes that recognized student voice as central to effective and meaningful learning processes. In his book *Freedom to Learn*,[1] humanist psychologist Carl Rogers also contributed to the movement through a person-based approach to education, noting how a safe, supportive environment allows each person to journey down the path of self-discovery, self-esteem, and self-directed learning. Recent research by Gary McPherson, Jane Davidson, and Robert Faulkner into the lives of more than 150 children, learning music from age seven to twenty-two, is noteworthy. They summarize their research in *Music In Our Lives*,[2] confirming the importance of student-centered teaching strategies as related to students' successful musical growth.

Teaching Tip

√ Engage students as whole persons through student-centered teaching.

1. Delve into and draw from students' personal lives.
2. Welcome students' active participation.
3. Do something about historical inequalities and privilege.

When teachers utilize student-centered teaching strategies, they delve into and draw from students' personal lives. They welcome students' active participation as persons whose collective thoughts, intellect, feelings, intuitions, and preferences undoubtedly influence their unfolding musical journey. They recognize how inequalities and privilege throughout history have impacted students based on their race, socioeconomic standing, gender, and culture.

In forthcoming chapters, *More than Music Lessons* makes important contributions to student-centered teaching by exploring the personal philosophy and practical tools for working with music students as genuine individuals. However, to be sure, a student-centered approach should not be interpreted as a stand-alone strategy for music instruction. The point is that meaningful music teaching weaves together two vital perspectives. On the curriculum-based side, teachers share their musical experience with students. On the student-centered side, teachers respectfully engage the breadth and depth of students' personal and musical realms.

Your Thoughts

More than Music Lessons presents a student-centered approach to teaching as it differs from curriculum-based instructional approach.

1. What does this difference mean to you?

2. Why is a student-centered approach an important aspect in today's music teaching environment?

CURRICULUM MODELS

Having worked with teachers over many years, I've noticed that how they teach is greatly influenced by the curriculum they employ. For example, take a look at the following four curriculum models and consider how students may benefit or be challenged by their teacher's choice of curriculum model:

1. Teacher-led curriculum is characterized by a formal, predetermined approach that guides student musical development from beginner to advanced levels. Examples of teacher-led curriculum include established sequential series like the Suzuki method and RCM (Royal Conservatory of Music) exams.
2. Student-led curriculum puts students in charge of their own musical journey. Examples include amateurs who take interest in their instrument as an adult, experienced teen students with adequate basic music competencies, and beginner students whose musical interests are driven by their influential music environment.
3. Student-sensitive curriculum is sensitive to students with special learning needs. Here, teachers typically modify an established instructional series so that students may progress at a slower pace and through more manageable steps.
4. Shared curriculum is characterized by the blending of a teacher-led curriculum (also student-sensitive) with a student-led curriculum. Here, the emphasis on sharing means both teachers and students have meaningful input. For example, teachers choose 50 percent of material and students also choose 50 percent.

Your Thoughts

Curriculum models: teacher-led curriculum, student-led curriculum, student-sensitive curriculum, shared curriculum.

1. Which of the above curriculum models describe your teaching approach?
2. Why is that the case? What are your reasons for choosing your curriculum model?

Over the expanse of my forty-year teaching career, it's interesting to note how my teaching has experienced all of the above curriculum models. During the first two decades of teaching, I consistently helped my students achieve musical success through a teacher-led curriculum (most often) and a student-sensitive curriculum (when appropriate). And I would probably still be teaching that way, except through a combination of various events, students, colleagues, and parents, I gradually shifted to a shared-curriculum approach. For me, using a shared curriculum makes total sense because it allows me to pass on my musical experience and at the same time actively engage students in exploring their own musical interests. As a result, my teaching looks quite different today as demonstrated in the following student examples.

From MBT's Studio

James: All through elementary school, I used a shared curriculum with James. Satisfied with his own musical competency in junior high, James gradually shifted to a student-led curriculum. For his final years of high school, James made all repertoire choices on his own. My role was to assist him with working out the details in terms of knowledge, skills, and resources he couldn't uncover on his own.

Janice: Similar to her brother James, I used a shared curriculum with Janice all through elementary school. However, in junior high and high school, Janice preferred to continue with a shared curriculum. She appreciated my choosing repertoire that suited her personality and technique. I appreciated her passion for movie themes.

Arthur: Once again, I used a shared curriculum with Arthur all through elementary school. In junior high, Arthur decided he wanted to complete three upper level RCM exams. This meant switching to a teacher-led curriculum for the eight months of preparation needed. After each exam, we continued with several months of shared curriculum.

Peter and Gloria: Building on the foundation of a student-sensitive curriculum (Peter has physical limitations and Gloria has mental development challenges), I use a shared-curriculum to ensure their journey has relevant input from both teacher and student.

I have an immense appreciation for a shared curriculum as my preferred modus operandi. This model offers the foundation of breadth and flexibility needed to ensure that both my students and I make vital contributions to their musical journey. With a shared curriculum, we learn to trust and value each other's input. Students learn they may rely on me for what I have to offer, and I learn so much about their own musical voice. When we need to change things up—with a teacher-led curriculum, student-sensitive curriculum, or a student-led curriculum—we've established the practical framework for how we'll respectfully continue to work together.

Why did I start out with a teacher-led curriculum for the first twenty years of my career? My impression is that for most teachers, a teacher-led curriculum is typically their first choice because it has been the dominant mode of instruction for more than two hundred years. We all know what a teacher-led curriculum looks like, and we know its strengths, so it's natural that teachers would make such a choice. The challenge is that teachers' strong commitment to a teacher-led curriculum and its track record of success may blind teachers to its personal and social impact. When teachers look more closely, they may observe how a teacher-led curriculum actually inhibits their capacity for responding to student inclusion and diversity. To be sure, although a teacher-led curriculum may meet certain students' musical interests, this approach may prove unsatisfactory across today's demographic landscape.

Depending on teachers' choice of curriculum model, it seems certain that their capacity for responding to diversity and inclusion may be enhanced or compromised as a result. For example, students with strong internal motivations to pursue their own personal or cultural directions may not be served well by a teacher-led curriculum. They may feel completely unrecognized by the focus on predetermined musical outcomes. Elsewhere, students attempting to complete formalized music requirements may not be served well by a student-led curriculum. For example, a student who wants to audition for an academic music program may struggle because there's simply too much they cannot figure out on their own.

Teaching Tip

√ Align curriculum model to meet with students' musical aspirations.

1. Make students' musical journey a shared experience.
2. Lead when necessary.
3. Provide resources students can't uncover on their own.
4. Be sensitive to students' learning needs.

I appreciate how music teaching may have arrived at a crossroads where it's possible to evaluate different curriculum models for their benefits and disadvantages; where it's possible to imagine teaching with different curriculum models in mind. In today's context, what seems desirable is that teachers genuinely align their curriculum with the aspirations students bring to their musical journey.

TEACHING FOR INCLUSION AND DIVERSITY

Twenty-first-century music instructors work in a demographic landscape of unprecedented diversity and richness. Questions that today's music teachers may face include: How can we be inclusive regarding the immense diversity of students in our population? What strategies will help us with meeting the needs of sectors that historically have encountered inequalities based on their race, socioeconomic standing, gender, and culture? Let's step back for a moment to consider the significance of the culturally diverse communities within which music education takes place.

Your Thoughts

Twenty-first-century music teachers work with an increasingly diverse student demographic.

1. How do you feel about working with increasing diversity in your studio?
2. Where are your challenges? Where are your successes?

In an era that asks music teachers to be attentive to diversity, equity, accessibility, and inclusion, they need to gain knowledge about cultural diversity that go beyond mere awareness, respect for, and recognition of the fact that ethnic groups have different values or express similar ones in various ways. Culture encompasses many aspects, some of which are more important than others because they have direct implications for teaching and learning. With factual information about cultural particularities regarding communication and relational patterns, teachers can adjust their instructional approach to match with their students' cultural background.

Culturally responsive teachers know how to determine the strengths and weaknesses of curriculum designs and instructional materials and make changes to improve their overall quality. To make music lessons a meaningful reflection of the communities they serve, teachers must be willing to disrupt the self-perpetuating cycle of traditional music education centered on Eurocentric musical ideals. Expanding the scope of repertoire to include music from students' own experience sends an important message: that students' musical interests matter and are valued.

Pedagogic conversations on the topic of culturally responsive teaching have been instrumental in drawing attention to the historical, social, and economic inequities since the 1990s[3] with more recent additions in the last decade.[4] According to Geneva Gay, culturally responsive teaching is defined as using the cultural characteristics, experiences, and perspectives of ethnically diverse students as conduits for teaching them more effectively.[5] This instructional approach is based on the idea that knowledge and skills situated within students' lived experiences and frames of references are perceived by students as more personally meaningful, have higher interest appeal, and are learned more easily and thoroughly. Culturally responsive teaching differs significantly from educational models in which ethnically diverse students forfeit their cultural background and psychological well-being in order to assimilate the dominant culture's preferred learning approach. What seems vital is that culturally responsive teachers take responsibility for the choices they make and the questions they ask themselves in order to meet the needs of an increasingly diverse generation of students.

Teaching Tip

√ Teach for inclusion and diversity.

1. Teachers reflect on their own upbringing.
2. Teachers take responsibility for learning about students, their culture, and communities.

Teaching for inclusion and diversity in the twenty-first century begins with teachers reflecting on their own upbringing and the values that their family and community have passed down. This process allows teachers to acknowledge their own culture and consider how it differs from their students. For example, Carrie Shearer[6] points out noticeable cultural differences related to silence in conversations. According to Shearer, many Asians are comfortable with a minute or two of silence, while Canadians and Americans are generally uncomfortable with more than a second of silence in conversations. This is exaggerated in Italian and Latin American cultures where people often interrupt or talk over each other, so there is never silence. In many Asian countries, it is considered polite to pause for a few seconds before answering a question to show that you have reflected upon the question and your response. In contrast are many Western countries where silence is viewed as a void that must be filled. Since silence has different meanings, it's important to decode it in each cultural context.

To make instruction relevant to students, teachers need to think about the way students learn and not get stuck in the way they have learned. According to Zaretta Hammond,[7] it's about building the learning capacity of the individual student by leveraging the affective and cognitive scaffolding that they bring with them. This means teachers need to recognize pedagogical practices taken for granted that might privilege some students over others. They need exemplary music knowledge and skills that inform how they deliver this content to culturally diverse students. Culturally responsive music teachers understand the role of culture in education and society.[8] They deliver instruction in a caring manner, as Karin Hendricks describes in her book *Compassionate Music Teaching*,[9] through the dynamics of trust, empathy, patience, inclusion, community, and authentic connection. Culturally responsive teaching is not a quick fix or simple strategy to add to teaching. This process takes reflection on an ongoing basis and a commitment to support students—even if it means teachers getting outside their cultural comfort zone.

What seems compelling is how teaching for inclusion and diversity encompasses small but well-placed steps that break down inequities resulting from centuries of colonization, prejudice, and injustice. To be sure, it is a giant undertaking for music teachers. Using a framework that addresses music teaching in terms of parents, practicing, projects, and character may offer fresh ground for getting things underway. By establishing learning environments that welcome conversations, questions, and stories of multiple voices, music teachers can set in motion reflective thoughts and actions, purpose and relationships to create a safe, welcoming, and inclusive music education community for everyone. With music as a catalyst for personal expression and social change, it should come as no surprise that music shines like a light at the end of the tunnel.

Build On and Exercise What's Already There

Student-centered teaching. Curriculum models. Teaching for inclusion and diversity.

1. How do you incorporate student-centered principles in your teaching?
2. How does your choice of curriculum model resonate with notions of inclusion and diversity?
3. What aspects of your curriculum model may actually privilege some students over others?

NOTES

1. Carl Rogers and H. Jerome Freiberg, *Freedom to Learn,* third edition (New York: Macmillan College Publishing Company, 1994).
2. G. E. McPherson, J. W. Davidson, and R. Faulkner, *Music in Our Lives* (Oxford, UK: Oxford University Press, 2012).
3. See Gloria Ladson-Billings, "Toward a Theory of Culturally Relevant Pedagogy," *American Education Research Journal* 32, no. 3 (1995): 465–91.
4. See Cathy Benedict, Patrick Schmidt, Gary Spruce, and Paul Woodford, *The Oxford Handbook of Social Justice in Music Education* (New York: Oxford University Press, 2015); Gholdy Muhammad, *Cultivating Genius: An Equity Framework for Culturally and Historically Responsive Literacy* (New York: Scholastic, 2020).
5. Geneva Gay, "Preparing for Culturally Responsive Teaching," *Journal of Teacher Education* 53, no. 106 (2002): 106–16.
6. Carrie Shearer, *The Cultural Implications of Silence Around the World* (2020), accessed May 1, 2021, https://www.rw-3.com/blog/cultural-implications-of-silence.
7. Zaretta Hammond, *Culturally Responsive Teaching and the Brain: Promoting Authentic Engagement and Rigor Among Culturally and Linguistically Diverse Students* (Thousand Oaks, CA: Corwin Press, 2015).
8. V. R. Lind and C. McKoy, *Culturally Responsive Teaching in Music Education* (New York: Taylor and Francis, 2016).
9. Karin Hendricks, *Compassionate Music Teaching* (London: Rowman & Littlefield, 2018).

Part 1

PARENTS

Music dances in our fingertips.

Music lives in our breath,
in our boldness, our whispers, our sighs.

Music grabs on without being asked.
It quickens our step
prompting vast internal awakenings.
It softens our gaze
recalling sentiments in melodies past.

Music brings light to shadowed stillness
illuminating imaginations with
beams of hope and love.

Familiar refrains speak to us
about solitude, about communion,
about the realness of where we are.

Music holds us in all our nakedness
at the furthest edges of our humanity
in the innermost resonance of our being.

Our enduring companion.
Our welcome friend.

Always music...

Chapter 2

Parents Make a Difference

From MBT's Studio

When I began music teaching during the late 1970s, the idea of parental involvement never occurred to me. Having grown up in an era when parents dropped off their children for music lessons, it seemed completely natural to continue with my own teacher's proven routine. Then everything changed in September 1980. Parents in a travelling Australian family indicated interest in helping with their sons' lessons and the colleague with whom I shared my teaching studio informed me of her success with parental involvement. It was a classic lightbulb moment that compelled me to telephone the parents of my beginner students. "I've noticed that when you help your child at home, things go better," I said. "If you want to sit in on the lesson every once in a while, that would be great." So, without any real preparation on my part, parents began attending their child's piano lessons. From time to time at first, and then, with relaxed regularity.

Looking back forty years later, I'm filled with gratitude that, quite serendipitously, I became aware of the difference parents can make in their child's musical development. Up until that time, I'd purposely kept parents at a distance because I worried they'd find fault with my limited teaching experience. Any thoughts about parents' positive impact on their child's music studies were blocked by my own insecurity as a teacher. As weeks and months passed, I realized that my worries were completely unsubstantiated. When parents attended, the lessons were about their child, not me. How could I have missed something so basic? Shifting my teaching approach to include parents set in motion a desire to better understand what parental involvement was all about. In the process, it triggered a deep respect for the complexity and intensity of every family's home life.

Your Thoughts

In part 1, we explore the topic of "parents."

1. What questions come to mind when you think about parents and music lessons?
2. What do you hope to take away from part 1?

Music education research provides compelling evidence that parents' interest and involvement in their child's musical study has a positive impact on student achievement, regardless of parental expertise in the field of music.[1] Parental support is consistently recognized, and encouraged, as providing an effective influence on children's motivation, involvement, persistence, and ongoing musical commitment. I believe that for most music teachers, the influence of parental interest may not come as a surprise. Looking back on my own childhood experiences, it's easy for me to recognize how my parents' casual and ongoing interest influenced what I accomplished musically and elsewhere. Their support made a noticeable difference without controlling or overtaking my own journey.

What can music teachers do to connect meaningfully with the complexity and intensity of every family's home life? My impression is that it starts with the instructional philosophy behind *More than Music Lessons*—that teachers build on and exercise what's already there. This means teachers taking the time to better understand the dynamics of family home life[2] and examine how music is woven into the fabric of every family's personal and interpersonal cultural setting.

FAMILY HOME LIFE

Every family's home life is a synthesis of activities and investments. With unconditional love as the driving undercurrent, parents make immense commitments to care for their children by providing energy, time, and finances. Conversations play a key role. Also silent moments spent alone and together. Meals need to be eaten. Proper clothing is a must. Good health means paying attention to adequate amounts of exercise, sleep, and cleanliness. There are times when fatigue, frustration, and crises produce setbacks. Values, beliefs, and traditions keep the ball rolling. Physical, emotional, and spiritual supports provide shelter and security. Music reaches across personal and family contexts. Education and entertainment make days go by quickly. Obviously, there's a lot going on in every family's home.[3]

Parents and children give shape to a family through their individual character and the relationships they have with each other. Each parent and child have their own independent identity with its own unique intensity, predispositions, and lifeline, which in turn influences how family relationships form and interact with one another.

Your Thoughts

Every family's home life is shaped by parents' and children's individual character and the relationships they have with each other.

1. What does the above statement mean to you?
2. How would you describe your family's home life?

Parents bring to family life their own well-established dispositions and experiences. They embody a history of personal philosophies and instinctive insights anchored by who they are as individuals. Parents also manage obligations such as employment, partner needs, community commitments, and household responsibilities. Their hopes and concerns are spread broadly. Their personal goals and needs are entwined with those for their children. Childrearing covers a wide timespan that includes the immediacy of their children's daily needs to preparing them for the future and immersing them in a well-rounded life.

Children also possess their own well-defined character. As early as infancy, a child's disposition is evident. They thrive in safe environments that offer protection yet allow them opportunities to learn from making good and bad choices. Children, like their parents, want autonomy in making independent explorations of the world and of themselves. Parents are key in helping children achieve confidence, resiliency, a sense of purpose and involvement, meaningful outcomes in all they do, a deep sense of self-worth, and the ability to handle life's adversities.

Teaching Tip

√ Everyone wants to be valued for who they are and what they do.

1. Students want to be valued for who they are and what they do.
2. Parents want to be valued for who they are and what they do.
3. Teachers want to be valued for who they are and what they do.

Despite obvious differences in identity and life experience, parents and children share a crucial commonality. Both parents and children want to be recognized for who they are. They want relationships with people who appreciate them for their individuality and not for what others expect them to be and do. Parents and children want to know they're valued and understood. No matter the child's temperament, age, personality, strengths, or weaknesses, parents do what they can to meaningfully address their child's best interests. Parents lead the way and they follow their child's lead. They support and encourage independence and ownership. They validate their child's achievements. However, acting in a child's best interests doesn't mean indulging their every whim. It also means being assertive in those things that are not negotiable. Parents allow their child to experience failure and the give-and-take associated with independence and ownership. They provide wise advice. Responding to the "best interest" of a child doesn't refer to an isolated, immovable, or perfect scenario that has no relation to the real world. Nor is that parents always get it right. When parents know better, they do better. Acting in the best interest of a child is no easy task. It's akin to a juggler attempting to keep in the air an iceberg, a cloud, and a glass of water all at the same time.

Often, parents may be the under-appreciated stewards of their child's best interest, rarely receiving thanks for their efforts. No other person takes on a child's best interest in the fundamental way parents do. Unlike other family members or teachers who may know a child from a distance, parents know their child from the fullness of their family's home life. Parents are their children's first model of human behavior. Through their parents' actions, children learn to be kind, considerate, honest, authentic, and caring. Regrettably, children may also learn about shame, fear, and control from what their parents do.

Most parents appreciate their children's individuality, what they have to say, and how they think. They help create positive memories for their children that often last a lifetime. They show their children that they love them every day. Nothing compares to parents' relationship with their children when it comes to positive influences. So, it's no surprise that parents' interest and support have a favorable impact on their children's musical development, even when parents have no musical knowledge.

MUSIC AND FAMILY HOME LIFE

Music provides a flexible and diverse means for supporting and developing parents' and children's individual identities and relationships. University researchers Diana Boer and Amina Adubakar found that music remains an important part of family dynamics, a way of transmitting family values and norms, and enhances family cohesion.[4] It serves as an important vehicle for maintaining communication, relationships, and a social activity for sharing emotions. The prevalence of music in a family's home contributes to the creation, maintenance, and retrieval of parents' and children's autobiographical memories. Music, as described by music researcher Anita Collins,[5] is a fundamental part of being human and our world is full of music. Musical experiences are important in how we develop understanding of the world right from birth.

Family-based opportunities such as performing, listening, and talking about music are plentiful. Listening to music, whether alone or with others, prompts rewarding physical and emotional effects on family members. Music may accompany work or study, provide distraction, relieve tension, and activate focus. Music is played in TV shows, advertising, and the movies. Just think of the musical themes from the movies *Star Wars* or *Jaws* and what they communicate or how music changes the dynamics of a sporting event. During family events like birthdays, holidays, weddings, funerals, and graduations, music provides a kind of official confirmation of the event's status. A birthday isn't complete without someone singing "Happy Birthday to You." Music also carries cultural and societal meanings for families through religious music, rap and hip-hop, musical theatre, popular and folk music for example. Through music, parents and children have the opportunity to explore and express a breadth of personal, family, and cultural values.

Your Thoughts

Music is woven into the fabric of every family's home life as a personal, family, and cultural value.

1. In what ways was music woven into the fabric of your own family's home life?
2. How did music in your family's home life influence your own musical development?

Music is a constant in the home life of most families. It isn't something stored away waiting for music lessons to begin. It's a vibrant part of parents' and children's daily life. Similarly, the dynamics of students' family home life are also a factor in their musical development. Whether students have completed five weeks or five years of music lessons, the influence of a family's home musical life is undeniable, along with parent/child identity and relationships, and parents' keeping the best interest of their child in mind. When teachers respect the dynamics of a student's family home musical life, they recognize that music teaching strategies must connect meaningfully with student's personal, family, and cultural values.

TEACHERS AND FAMILY HOME LIFE

From ancient times to modern days, teachers have held an esteemed social status based on their role as knowledgeable and experienced resources and on expertise in their respective domain. Throughout the ages, people have sought out teachers' guidance because they recognize teachers have the capacity to remove the guesswork from science, sports, mathematics, arts, and more. Teachers put students on a path to successful learning by ensuring that they gain knowledge that will guide them in the right direction. Teachers pass on their expertise, foster the continuation of traditions, and ensure the next generation's development of excellence. Yet the process of teaching is a great deal more than just telling others what to do, or passing on what they know, or turning students into replications of themselves. So what's missing? What else is there? The answer is that teachers have respect for what's already there.

Teachers weave two meaningful layers into the fabric of their teaching. On one layer, we find teachers sharing with others what they know. That's why we depend on them. In the other layer, we see teachers showing respect for students' family home life. Teachers recognize that music lessons are only a small part of the enormous world that is a student's musical life. They teach beyond the music lesson.

From MBT's Studio

The Fletcher family lived forty-five minutes outside the city. The children were home-schooled to allow time for their participation in competitive ice hockey. Somehow, they managed to fit in music lessons. On weeks when it seemed like they would spend more time in the car than anywhere else, we used available technology to connect via online lessons. My role as teacher was to help with students' musical development by building on their family home life.

Long before students begin music lessons, we know their family home musical life is already present no matter how casual, eccentric, stereotypical, predictable, or random. What happens when music teachers respect their students' family home musical life? Instead of trying to control students' family life or impose their own vision of the ideal musical environment, the concept of respect means teachers genuinely connect with the family home music life that's already there. Teachers develop relationships with parents based on understanding, acceptance,[6] care,[7] cultural responsiveness,[8] diversity, and inclusion.[9] In this context, teachers operate as collaborative resources who ask "not what parents can do for them, but rather what they can do for parents."[10] Rather than treating parents, students, and family life with a list of obligations and expectations, respect means teachers get to work with what's already in place. They're curious without being intrusive, invitational without being patronizing. They make meaningful connections because they know students' family home life will have a grounding and ongoing impact on students' musical development in the weeks, months, and years to come.

Teaching Tip

√ Respect every student's family home life.

1. Engage with what's already there.
2. Make meaningful connections.

The human condition is one of relationships, whether it's with a community or a nation. We live in relationships and thrive in relationships based on respect for one another. Not merely respect for what we might want to see in someone else, but respect for the life that person genuinely leads. Respect is a gift teachers, students, and parents share with each other. When music teachers respect their students' home musical life, they fulfill a connectedness most basic to our humanity: the capacity to listen to each other with open hearts and minds, not for control or competition. They listen for insight and relationship. Music teachers may create appreciative, understanding, and caring spaces by respectfully building on and exercising the family home musical life that's already there.

INDEPENDENCE AND OWNERSHIP

Knowing that music teaching strategies must connect meaningfully with students' family home musical life, it's interesting to consider how teachers and parents may support or facilitate the notion of personal independence in their child. The following episode from my early years of teaching is an example of the concerns parents may bring forward.

From MBT's Studio

"So, just how long will it be before my child is able to practice on his own?" This question from a student's father was direct and to the point. It made me realize that I needed to think about how my teaching would address the fundamental dynamics of student independence and ownership. "Well, I think you'll be pleasantly surprised to see how many things your child can do on his own even after the very first lesson!" I replied. Obviously, this father was standing up for the best interests of his child and I could certainly support him and his child in that direction.

It's remarkable just how much this father's question of more than three decades ago influenced the trajectory of my teaching. Namely, that I deliberately set up my teaching approach to accommodate and promote the notion of personal independence. I could see that independence was something parents understand from the moment of their child's birth. No matter how much planning or scheduling parents do, their child always responds as an independent individual. This view of independence also matched my own experience of growing up and living as an adult. My instructional approach would thrive best when it synchronized with parents' value of raising independent children because learning to sing or play a musical instrument is a great way for students to invest in their capacity for independence and for parents to support their child's experience of independence in a safe environment. So, I replied in support of the father's awareness of independence and the child's natural indications for independence, and made a strong mental note to ensure that my instructional approach encouraged students' independence and ownership from the very first lesson.

Observe how the phrase "Make sure you . . . " takes on differing emphases of independence and ownership in the following scenarios:

Scenario 1: After an important instructional exchange, the teacher turns to the student and says, "Make sure you show your dad how to do this when you get home." (Student has ownership.)

Scenario 2: After an important instructional exchange, the teacher turns to the student and says, "I want to make sure you practice this section properly when you get home." (Teacher has ownership.)

Scenario 3: After an important instructional exchange, the teacher turns to the parent and says, "Make sure your son completes this assignment when you get home." (Parent has ownership.)

My goal in teaching is to incorporate language and gestures that put students in charge. That means I'm careful not only about the words I use, I'm also careful about the person I'm addressing.

Teaching Tip

√ Exercise students' independence and ownership.

1. Parents know about their child's independence from birth.
2. Use language and gestures that synchronize with raising independent children.
3. Be prepared to go slowly.

What happens when students take charge in an incorrect way? For example, what do I do when the student makes a recurring error? Do I tell the parent to correct the error or do I invite the student to shed light on the learning process? Either way, there will be an adjustment to the error but only one action will reinforce the student's independence and ownership. Asking the parent to make the adjustment may be faster to implement. However, my role as a teacher isn't just to find the fastest way to solve student challenges. My role is to incorporate teaching processes—slowing down if necessary—and find the most deliberate way for students to take ownership of their learning process. Does that mean lessons always go according to the student independence and ownership plan?

Unfortunately, lessons may occasionally go in directions I least expect, like when I ask the student for permission to invite parental assistance and the student says, "No, I don't want any help." On the one hand, the student might be saying, "I don't need any help." The student might be confident of handling things without assistance, so I respect the input. After all, there is nothing to lose by seeing what the student can independently accomplish in one week. On the other hand, the student might be saying, "My dad makes me nervous when he helps out." This is a signal that the parent's involvement might benefit from either the teacher's or student's input.

The following scenarios demonstrate the difference language and gestures can make between parents and students being in charge:

Scenario 1: Before the home practice session, the parent says to the student, "Let's get going. I've only got twenty minutes and we've got a lot to get done today in your practice." (Parent is pressed for time and in charge.)

Scenario 2: Before the home practice session, the parent says to the student, "What was the name of your favorite piece yesterday? It would be so fun to start with a concert performance?" (Parent is relaxed and ready for the student to take charge.)

Scenario 3: During the home practice session, the parent says to the student, "I want to see if you remember the important point about the bow." (Parent is in charge.)

Scenario 4: During the home practice session, the parent says to the student, "I can't remember what the teacher said about your bow hold. Something about the pinky? Could you teach me?" (Parent is interested in the student taking charge.)

Obviously, language and gestures count a lot in parents' support of their child's independence. Why might parents forget about their child's independence? Multiple factors come to mind. Parents are busy. They may unknowingly hold onto expressions from their past. Parents may be unaware of the impact from their words or actions.

Teaching Tip

√ Encourage parents to use language and gestures that put their child in the leadership role.

1. Remember that parents may not have critical awareness of their words or actions.
2. Proceed gently and respectfully.
3. Allow parents to compare different approaches.

Why are parents so adept at supporting independence? While we might consider the role of unconditional love or the influence of social contexts, I believe there's another angle to consider. Parents know what it's like to experience independence and ownership for themselves. They know the joy, satisfaction, empowerment, sense of meaning and confirmation of self-esteem that comes with independence and ownership. Parents also know what it's like to have independence and ownership taken away, to be denied independence, to have ownership go unrecognized. Music teachers can go a long way in demonstrating, raising awareness, and reminding parents of the benefits that come with consistently nurturing their child's independence and ownership.

Your Thoughts

This chapter included the Teaching Tip, "Everyone wants to be valued for who they are and what they do."

1. What does this statement mean to you?
2. How is this statement evident in your teaching?

NOTES

1. See also: B. Bloom, *Developing Talent in Young People* (New York: Ballantine Books, 1985); A. Creech, "The Role of the Family in Supporting Learning," in *The Oxford Handbook of Music Psychology,* edited by S. Hallam and I. T. Cross (Oxford: UK: Oxford University Press, 2009), 295–306; J. Davidson, M. Howe, and J. Sloboda, "The Role of Parents in the Success and Failure of Instrumental Learner," *Bulletin of the Council for Research in Music Education* 127 (1995): 40–44; G. McPherson and J. Davidson, "Playing an Instrument," in *The Child as Musician* edited by G. McPherson (Oxford, UK: Oxford University Press, 2006), 331–51; A. Nathan, *The Music Parents' Survival Guide: A Parent-to-parent Conversation* (Oxford, UK: Oxford University Press, 2014); R. Cutietta, *Raising Musical Kids: A Guide for Parents* (Oxford, UK: Oxford University Press, 2013); A. Gonzalez-DeHass, P. Willems, and M. Doan Holbein, "Examining the Relationship Between Parental Involvement and Student Motivation," *Educational Psychology Review* 17 (2005): 99–123.

2. The descriptor "family home life" is an overarching term not intended as an idealized interpretation. Regrettably, students may come from broken families and difficult situations. Taking the time to understand students' personal context is important.

3. Similarly for college and adult music students, there's a lot going on in their daily lives that has an impact on their musical development.

4. D. Boer and A. Abubakar, "Music Listening in Families and Peer Groups: Benefits for Young People's Social Cohesion and Emotional Well-being Across Four Cultures," *Frontiers in Psychology* 5 (May 8, 2014): 392.

5. Anita Collins, *The Music Advantage: How Music Helps Your Child Develop, Learn, and Thrive* (New York: TarcherPerigree, 2021).

6. C. Rogers and H. J. Freiberg, *Freedom to Learn,* third edition (New York: Macmillan College Publishing Company, 1994).

7. Nel Noddings, *The Challenge to Care in Schools: An Alternative Approach to Education* (New York: Teachers College Press, 2005).

8. G. Gay, "Preparing for Culturally Responsive Teaching," *Journal of Teacher Education* 53 no. 106 (2002): 106–16.

9. Karin S. Hendricks, *Compassionate Music Teaching (*London, UK: Rowman & Littlefield, 2018).

10. G. L. Rudney, *Every Teacher's Guide to Working with Parents* (Thousand Oaks, CA: Corwin Press, 2005).

Chapter 3

In the Lesson

STEP IN, STEP BACK, LET GO

In order for teachers to make meaningful connections between parents, students' family home musical life, and music lessons, it may be advantageous for teachers to consider questions like, "How can I help parents move through the various stages of their child's musical development?" "When is right time to step in?" "When is it appropriate to step back?" "When should I let go?" Take a look at the following.

Teacher	*Parent*
Mr. Benedict typically starts violin beginner students anywhere between the ages of five and nine. His primary focus is to help children experience independence and ownership from Day One. He encourages parents of younger children to attend lessons and practice with their child at home. With older children who begin lessons on their own, he puts them immediately in charge and writes notes for home practice. He emphasizes frequent listening to the repertoire recording. He writes report cards at each term's end to share with parents.	Mrs. Bell enrolled her son in violin lessons at five years of age. She attended her son's lessons and recorded the notes Mr. Benedict dictated during the lesson. She assisted her son's practice often from the kitchen or her computer. She played the recording from time to time and gradually found her way with validating her son's independence. Mrs. Bell appreciated the one-on-one parent/teacher interview at the end of each term.

When students have completed the ear-based stage of learning (6 months to 2 years), Mr. Benedict assists students transition to practicing on their own. To ensure students' growing competency, Mr. Benedict helps students gain proficiency with a variety of student practice tools (See Part 2: Practicing). He writes notes for their home practice. As some weeks go better than others, Mr. Benedict maintains a fluid approach that allows for ebb and flow of excellence. He continues with report cards and end of term parent meetings.	Between seven and eight years of age, Mr. Benedict suggested Mrs. Bell begin stepping back to allow her son to practice on his own—albeit some weeks were better than others. Mr. Benedict wrote notes to guide her son's practice. She drove her son to his lesson and waited for him outside his teacher's studio. She played the repertoire recording after prompting by her son's teacher. She routinely praised her son for taking charge and made requests for impromptu concert performances. She appreciated checking in with Mr. Benedict at the end of term meetings.
As students progress through the repertoire, Mr. Benedict understands that students easily adopt and forget the tools of effective home practice as they acquire new pieces. He uses a cyclical approach to address "big picture" and "detailed" views of instruction in each lesson. Report cards and parent meetings continue.	By eleven years of age, Mrs. Bell's son could organize most of his own practicing and listening to the recording—still with some weeks better than others. It made a huge difference when she praised him for his independence especially when he got discouraged. Mrs. Bell appreciated checking with Mr. Benedict at the end of term meetings.
Mr. Benedict understands that junior high and high school students have a lot on their plate. He is strategic in planning for RCM exams, concerts, and special projects (See Part 3: Projects). Report cards and parent meetings continue.	When Mrs. Bell's son entered junior high school, she realized she'd gotten out of the habit of requesting impromptu concert performances. Her requests proved to be just what her son needed. Mrs. Bell continued to check in with Mr. Benedict at term's end.
Mr. Benedict thinks it's important to celebrate students' musical journey with a final home concert that represents the student's own personal interests.	In Mrs. Bell's son's last year of high school, she enjoyed the small concert he prepared with his younger sister and two friends from his teacher's studio.

Mr. Benedict brings an entire journey's worth of organization and strategy to his violin students and their parents. For his students, he uses a step-by-step approach with lots of reminders, revisiting, and refinement to support them with the tools they'll need on their musical journey. With parents, he's sensitive to the evolving relationship they have with their child. He clearly explains to parents that he wants to avoid locking them into years of sitting down to practice every day with their child. He believes that the best thing he can do for parents is to help them modify their involvement to match their children's musical growth. He supports parents with guidance: when to step in to help, step back to allow for growth, and let go while remaining interested.

What's noteworthy is how stepping in, stepping back, and letting go can be applied in two distinct applications. As demonstrated in Mr. Benedict's approach, this framework can serve as a long-term strategy for evolving parental involvement applied over several years. As a short-term strategy, this framework also describes those impromptu moments when parents spontaneously appreciate their child's musical commitment. For example, when parents step in to request their independent ten-year-old for a spur-of-the-moment concert, or step back to sit quietly within view of their teenager's musical wanderings, or let go while continuing to offer words of encouragement given the demands their child faces in school and daily life. No matter the age or level of study, all children appreciate being valued by their parents.

Your Thoughts

Step In, Step Back, Let Go

1. What do you think of Step In, Step Back, Let Go as a strategy for parental involvement?
2. How does this strategy synchronize with what you're already doing?
3. What might you do differently?

This kind of parental involvement has a lot in common with parent-author Barbara Coloroso's message in her book *Kids Are Worth It*.[1] Coloroso encourages parents to let their children learn from real-life situations that are not life-threatening, morally threatening, or unhealthy. Under such conditions, children learn that they can make decisions and solve problems. By responding to real-life situations like learning to sing or play a musical instrument, children learn about the world around them and that they themselves have positive control over their own lives. Fortunately, there is nothing about music lessons that is life-threatening, morally threatening, or unhealthy. When students miss a day practicing, perform too quickly, or play wrong notes, they will most assuredly survive to play another day.

Teaching Tip

√ Help parents navigate their child's musical journey with Step in, Step back, and Let go.

1. Students' musical development occurs stage by stage.
2. Parents adapt to students' musical and personal growth.
3. Teachers keep parents informed through ongoing conversations, report cards, and parent meetings.

By contributing to a child's ownership of the most basic developmental stages like learning to walk or talk, parents solidify a key relational dimension: they unconditionally support the child's failures and celebrate the achievements. What stands out is how parents have the awareness and expertise to help their child navigate through various degrees of independence over the long term and in spontaneous moments. Parents know about the differences in their first child from their second. They recognize that supporting a seven-year-old's independence isn't the same as a teenager's. They know what's negotiable and what's not, when to push, when to pull, when hunger and fatigue may have implications. Therefore, it makes good sense for teachers to encourage parents' evolving participation in their child's musical journey.

DIVERSE FAMILY NEEDS

While parents aspire to do the best they can, they may also face numerous limitations in terms of resources and opportunities as well as handling multiple responsibilities and obligations of parenthood. Take a look at the following examples from the Johnson and Robinson families.

From MBT's Studio

A month after her five-year-old daughter Angela started lessons, Mrs. Johnson informed me, that for health reasons, she would be unable to attend Angela's lessons for one year. Every week, Angela's sixteen-year-old cousin drove her to her lessons. Angela practiced on her own at home. Once Mrs. Johnson's health improved, Angela continued to practice on her own because that was what she preferred. Years later, Angela informed me that her mom offered her an irresistible incentive as reward for her independent piano practicing: computer video games!

Mrs. Robinson's heavy work schedule made it impossible for her to regularly attend her two children's lessons. Accordingly, she enlisted her husband and the children's grandmother for assistance. Every week, someone different would bring the children for their lessons: mother, father, or grandmother. As the children's piano teacher, I was the consistent conduit, ensuring that mother, father, and grandmother could appreciate what was going on in the children's lessons. It was an extraordinary situation for these students to have the support of three keenly interested individuals.

Working with the Johnson and Robinson families, I learned that music lessons don't take place within an idyllic setting where everything revolves solely around prioritizing musical involvement. Music lessons take place within the reality of every family's home life and teachers possess the creativity, passion, and flexibility necessary to deliver engaging and meaningful musical instruction that supports students' independence and ownership under multiple conditions. While parents have an astounding amount of life experience to draw from in organizing their child's practice sessions, the limitations of a family's home life can make it difficult to attend lessons and practice with their children at home.

Teaching Tip

√ Make it work for real life families.

1. Find out what's already there.
2. Come up with multiple destinations and possible routes.
3. Be prepared for detours.

Teachers can welcome real-life families into the studio, along with their strengths and obstacles, rather than attempt to mold them into a teacher's "dream version" of family life. Meeting diverse family needs doesn't need to be a complicated, uncomfortable affair. It boils down to teachers finding out what's already there, figuring out what families need, and finding out what works, rather than attempting to reconfigure the family structure.

TAKING HOMEWORK NOTES

Taking homework notes during music lessons is a recognized and effective strategy for guiding a student's musical journey, yet there is considerable debate about who should do the note-taking. Is it the teacher's responsibility?

Should parents take notes so that teachers can save time and accomplish more? Are notes even necessary?

During my three-year teacher apprenticeship in Matsumoto, Japan, I had the opportunity to observe many student lessons on a daily basis. The following conversation took place when the mother of a student brought a tape recorder into the studio.

> Music teacher: Good afternoon. What's the tape recorder for?
>
> Mother: Oh, excuse me. We just want to be sure we can follow your instructions to the letter when we get home.
>
> Music teacher: That's admirable, but there are a few things you should know. Tape recording is wonderful, but it has its own problems. For example, when you get home, you'll be thinking that I said something during the lesson, and you'll spend the whole week looking for it when actually it was something I said last week or even several weeks ago. It might even be something you hoped I said, but actually didn't. And you spend the whole week looking for it. Next, you should know that I'm quite happy to make notes for you to take home. And there's no need for you to worry if by chance there's some detail missing—I'll be sure to include it next time. Anyway, what I hope you'll soon discover is that basically I say the same thing week after week. That I cycle through the same themes over and over. So, instead of worrying about every detail, just be here and appreciate your child.

As a university graduate who'd spent many years taking notes and following them to the letter, it's easy to see why this conversation impressed me. I assumed that note-taking was essential in ensuring that my students would know exactly what to do when they got home. Detailed, instructive homework notes would eliminate unnecessary detours on my students' musical journeys.

My takeaway from the above conversation is that music teachers are responsible for demystifying the layers that make teaching and learning work. On one hand, there's a broad, ongoing, cyclical quality in which teaching and learning return repeatedly to address the most fundamental topics: tone production, technique, beat and rhythm, intonation, breathing, reading and interpretation, theory and analysis, and more. This is the "big picture" of teaching and learning. On the other hand, there's the detailed adjustments and refinements to teaching and learning that, once again, cyclically address the most fundamental topics of tone production, etc. This is the close-up view of teaching and learning. Both are important, and getting too involved in one or the other can be problematic.

Your Thoughts

Homework notes play an integral role in guiding students at-home musical development.

1. Who takes the homework notes in your studio? Why?
2. What are the advantages and disadvantages of who takes the notes?

Who should make the homework notes? The options are teachers, parents, and students. What's most relevant is who has the knowledge and practical experience to determine what should be included in the notes. Teachers are best equipped to make notes because they obviously have more musical and instructional experience than parents or students. However, making notes has two important layers. Firstly, homework notes are intended to guide students' practice at home. Secondly, the actual process of making notes is important because it allows teachers to strengthen ideas with students that took place during the lesson and also to revisit these ideas with students at the lesson's conclusion. In this way, note-taking is a process that actively engages students throughout their lessons.

No matter who takes the homework notes, it's important for teachers to ensure the student is also engaged in the process. For example, when I take notes, I look for visual confirmation and verbal input from the child. In addition to providing explicit instructions, I might say something like, "What should I write in your notebook?" or "Which bar has the F sharp?" or "What challenge do you want to use?" In this way, I put students in charge. Similarly, when parents take notes, it's more about them recording the input from teacher and student than being tasked with figuring out what's going on. So, in addition to my own instructions, I might say to the student something like, "What should your dad write in your notebook?" or "Can you tell your mom which bar has the F sharp?" or "What challenge do you want your dad to put in the notes?" In this way, I reinforce the student's ownership of their own homework notes and avoid giving students the impression their parents are the ones in charge.

Teaching Tip

√ Provide teacher and student input for the person taking homework notes.

1. When parents take notes, thank them for being willing scribes.
2. Let parents retire from taking homework notes as part of "stepping back."

Finally, there is the question of having parents take notes in order to maximize time spent on more material or ideas during the lesson. My impression is that note-taking contributes to the ebb and flow of teaching and learning processes. Effective teaching and learning processes aren't the same as factory production schedules, which maximize efficiency at every moment. Effective processes have a fluidity to them that allows for intense moments of involvement followed by activities of less concentration. Teaching and learning benefit by alternating between focused attention and relaxed activities. Constant, focused learning may be counterproductive since the brain requires quiet periods to process newly obtained information. In other words, taking a few moments to take notes during the lesson gives students the space to readjust before continuing.

Your Thoughts

This chapter includes the Teaching Tip–"Make it work for real-life families."

1. What are the benefits and obstacles for teachers making it work for real-life families?
2. How is the notion of inclusion and diversity evident in your working with real-life families?

NOTE

1. Barbara Coloroso, *Kids Are Worth It: Giving Your Child the Gift of Inner Discipline* (Toronto, ON: Somerville House Publishing, 1995).

Chapter 4

Meaningful Conversations

PARENTS AND QUESTIONS

From MBT's Studio

> While six-year-old Christine is having her lesson, her father, Mr. Smith, watches with enthusiasm. Everything seems to be going as anticipated until, for some reason, Christine falters and an expression of disbelief spreads over her face. Inexplicably, she cannot find the first note. Mr. Smith turns with exasperation to the teacher and exclaims, "She played the entire piece perfectly yesterday! What on earth is going on?"

Questions such as Mr. Smith's are emotional and eruptive interrogations that can consume any parent's thinking process. Similarly, it's not unusual for students to express their own questioning and frustration when lesson performances display little of the expertise they experienced at home. Often, such questions arrive like a bolt of lightning, catching everyone off guard. And yet there is legitimacy to these questions that deserve thoughtful and purposeful deliberation. So, what do teachers do with such questions in the course of their teaching?

Parents have many questions concerning their child and the process of learning to sing or play a musical instrument. And, on occasion, those questions arise during the child's lesson. Parents have a powerful, emotional bond with their child and often can't stop themselves from asking these questions, hoping that the teacher's answers might shed light on what their child's learning process is all about. This means that I always respond to questions like Mr. Smith's during my students' lessons, knowing that if I don't or if I delay my answer to a later date, Mr. Smith may turn his question to the next available person, his six-year-old daughter Christine. It's not hard to imagine that during the car ride home following Christine's lesson, Mr. Smith would waste no time before grilling her on what had just happened during her lesson.

There is an entire classification of questions that plague educational processes like learning to sing or play a musical instrument. Such questions include, "Why do people play perfectly at home and make mistakes during their lessons?" and conversely, "Why do people make mistakes at home and play perfectly at their lessons?" Questions that connect with the conundrum "Why is it that people sometimes play perfectly without ever practicing, when on other occasions they completely fall apart?" Admittedly, the answers to these questions are complex. That's why I'm not fond of answers such as, "Don't worry. It happens to everybody" because dismissing the question is not an answer, and knowing that it happens to everyone is of little benefit when parents like Mr. Smith are genuinely searching for a solution.

My own understanding of learning processes has been greatly enhanced by the books *How We Learn* by Benedict Carey[1] and *Make It Stick* by Peter Brown, Henry Roediger, and Mark McDaniel.[2] What stands out for me is that our understanding of learning as some kind of linear process may not tell the entire story. That's not to say we shouldn't use linear processes in learning. Rather, it means that while linear processes dominate learning strategies, learning is actually more convoluted and less predictable than we think. Forgetting, hitting plateaus, confusion, and reworking are all part of learning even though our preference may be for the learning process to proceed logically and securely from one step to another. Research conducted by the above authors demonstrates how effective learning benefits from a diversity of learning challenges, which include mixing things up, embracing difficulties, spacing out activities, acknowledging forgetting, and allowing for incubation. Learning is more like exploring a vast network of interrelated and overlapping activities than simply climbing a ladder. So, when Mr. Smith reacts strongly to his daughter's learning efforts, it's time for me to step in with a more complete version of what's actually going on.

Teaching Tip

√ Make time to proactively address parents' concerns.

1. Be ready with your thoughts on important topics.
2. Be ready to listen.

As human beings, we are all creatures of habit who hope to live safe, secure, and steady lives with minimal setbacks or disruptions. We feel better when our lives include sufficient amounts of routine and dependability. Sleeping in the same bed, eating familiar foods, and socializing with a particular group—these are just a few of the routine habits that help create stability and contribute to our feelings of personal well-being. In processes like learning to sing or play a musical instrument, the problem is that our preference for security and dependability may mean we're ill-prepared when setbacks and disruptions appear. For example, parents may feel their attempts to create stability and safety in their child's lives are in jeopardy when their child doesn't want to practice or when their child's progress is inconsistent. They may think that if practicing went well yesterday, it's reasonable to anticipate a similar, positive continuation in today's practice, and tomorrow's practice should be even better. They may even think their child is doomed if they miss a day of practice. Before they know it, students' musical development may have more in common with a factory assembly line than with the ups and downs associated with achievement we know from real life. And parents may feel guilty when their child's musical journey lacks the well-intentioned expectations for security and dependability they had in mind. Yet, as evident in the above research, learning processes are much less predictable than we might prefer.

My responsibility to parents is to make sure they're equipped with an accurate understanding of real-life learning processes. It's an important conversation to have from the very beginning of their child's musical journey. And it's a topic that deserves frequent updating over the long trajectory of students continuing lessons. When things aren't going well at home, I want to know about it—not so I can keep an authoritarian control over parents and students, but so I may specifically tailor my contributions to their real-life context. On days when children don't want to practice, my advice for parents and students is to take the day off. Enjoy each other's company. No student's musical development will be shattered by missing a day of practice. Above all, I want to be certain that no parent or student leaves my studio feeling guilty about what they're doing at home.

What I appreciate about students, parents, and teachers coming together is the opportunity to share learning experiences with each other. That's why I welcome parents into the lesson environment, and I respond to questions like Mr. Smith's. It's also why I'm consistent in proactively addressing parents' concerns regarding the transition from ear-based learning to note reading, technical development, repetition, independence, and ownership. I take the time to listen and respond to parents' questions and concerns during their child's lessons—even though I know some music teachers will argue that parents should never interrupt the teacher. My experience has shown that a five-minute conversation with a parent can go a long way in working through their concerns.

Does that mean I spend all my time talking to parents during their child's lessons? Not in the least! However, it does mean that because I pay attention to parents' questions and routinely anticipate their concerns, I am able to offer advice as a natural occurrence, rather than as an intrusion into their child's lesson. In this way, parents' questions never get in the way of the child's learning process. More significantly, parents' questions contribute to everyone's understanding of what's involved in learning to sing or play a musical instrument.

Your Thoughts

Parents have questions.

1. What proactive mechanisms do you have in place to address parents' questions before their child begins lessons?
2. Make a list of questions that parents typically ask regarding elementary students. Include your answers for these questions.
3. Make a list of questions that parents typically ask regarding junior high and high school students. Include your answers for these questions.

ACCEPTABLE TENSION

Challenges related to parental involvement often emerge because parents regard music study as an activity their children ideally pursue as an intrinsic desire. Given the intimate nature of the parent/child relationship, it is not surprising that conflicts arise as a result of discrepancies between parental expectations and children's musical preferences or commitments to practice. Under such circumstances, as music educator Andrea Creech explains, "It is important for children to sustain a sense of being emotionally supported by their parents even in the face of disagreements."[3] Taking such interpersonal tensions into consideration, it is interesting to note how conflict's reputation is generally assumed to be a negative one. Conflict is interpreted as an obstacle to successful student achievement. It's a problematic aspect of learning to sing or play a musical instrument that, under ideal circumstances, should be minimized or avoided, if not completely eliminated. Yet in my own teaching, rather than categorically avoiding conflict, I carefully consider this instructional characteristic as a matter of *acceptable tension*. I draw on the value of conflict for its potential to contribute positively to successful student achievement.

Prominent academics John Dewey,[4] Leon Festinger,[5] and Daniel Berlyne[6] have established a clear link between dissonant experiences and learning development. They promote the idea that learning is often sparked by tensions that take us beyond our usual comfort zone. What I appreciate about the idea of *acceptable tension* is the reminder that learning to sing or play a musical instrument is not a smooth trajectory without its ups and downs. Musical exploration, study, and performance naturally involve conflict, upsets, tension, and opposition. My job as teacher is to ensure, as much as possible, that *tension* is always at an *acceptable* level, that disagreements are manageable, and that upsets get resolved so that learning to play a musical instrument remains satisfying, fun, and rewarding.

Teaching Tip

√ Support parents by shedding light on the
likelihood of acceptable tensions.

1. Make connections to the child's everyday life.
2. Ask parents to share their thoughts on acceptable tensions.
3. Acknowledge the achievements and setbacks
that accompany independence.

When it comes to parental involvement in their child's music studies, I realize that parents may encounter tension in reminding their child to practice. And, whereas many parents remain steadfast in reminding their child to do academic homework over a period of several years, the support they give their child in terms of musical practice tends to drop off toward the end of the child's first year of musical studies—at the very time they need ongoing parental encouragement to continue.[7] Yet music education research conducted by Andrea Creech clearly indicates that young children, adolescents, and teenagers alike value the support and interest of their parents.[8]

I want parents to understand that reminding their child to practice might be an example of acceptable tension that's in the best interest of their child. I want them to know some tensions are more valuable than others and being able to respond appropriately to tensions or conflicts is an essential component in children's learning about, and preparing for, the challenges of life. I encourage parents to figure out how acceptable tension fits in with who they are as parents and the vision they have of their child in adulthood. In this way, parental involvement is reflective of the values parents want to pass on to their child. It's not a sanitized problem-free process that occurs outside the realities of life. It is a journey in which students experience, respond to, and prepare for the acceptable tensions that come with the fullness of life.

Please note: Acceptable tensions should never be confused with "Tiger Mom" actions that use physical force, intimidation, degradation, shame, punishment, humiliation, or embarrassment to achieve musical ends. Acceptable tensions consistently prioritize the dignity and self-esteem of students, parents, and teachers. For an extensive examination of appropriate strategies, see chapters 7 and 9 in particular.

PARENTS' MOST PRACTICAL RESOURCE

From MBT's Studio

> At a music conference several years ago, I met with a cello instructor colleague for an informal conversation. When I asked her what stood out as a light bulb moment in her teaching that year, she replied, "I've noticed that the students, whose parents make friends with other parents in my studio, always seem to do well." I nearly fell over with astonishment having noticed precisely the same phenomenon in my own studio without ever making the connection between parent-peer relationships and student success.

My colleague's observation regarding parent-peer relationships made perfect sense because more than anyone else, another parent would understand the difficulties and the rewards of music study, even more than a teacher with parenting experience. Another parent would know what it feels like to overcome obstacles and celebrate a child's musical achievements. A parent-peer would more intuitively understand what it is like when children do not want to practice, when children declare they equally hate their instrument, their parents, and their music teachers.

Given that music teachers know a great deal about music, teaching, and the rigors involved in learning to sing or play a musical instrument for themselves, it seems logical that they would necessarily be parents' most practical resource. However, my experience in working with parents would indicate the contrary. This does not mean teachers have little to offer parents, rather parents' practical needs may be more closely aligned with a resource other than teachers as the above conversation illustrates.

Iscoe and Bordelon explain that parent-peer relationships seem to provide the one thing that is beyond professionals in any field: another parent who understands.[9] Parent-peers fill a much-needed role that adds an important dimension to parents' relationships with and understanding of their child by offering practical resources for them that address areas outside the experience of teacher professionals. This sentiment is echoed in Bell, Fitzgerald, and Legge's acknowledgment that parent-peers provide the most valuable assistance by listening and offering "an informed, experience-based perspective."[10]

Teaching Tip

√ Peers are parents' most practical resource.

1. Schedule regular opportunities for parent-peer relationships to develop.
2. Provide a separate physical space for parents to talk.
3. Use available video conference technology when appropriate.

Recognizing that parents need recurring opportunities to develop friendships with other parents, I make sure they get to know each other by deliberately introducing them to each other and encouraging them to exchange contact information: it only takes a matter of seconds at the end of a group class or at a concert. I continually reinforce the resource they are for each other, emphasizing how one parent's insight has meaning for another and how parent-peer conversations will twist and turn through matters important to them that I cannot foresee. Today's parents also have an enormous number of resources to draw from thanks to the internet, social media, and texting. With extensive online peer communities including Facebook groups, Instagram hashtags, and more, parents have many ways to gather information and share experiences in addition to in-person communication.

From MBT's Studio

Prior to the first group class, I explained to Mrs. Oliver that her daughter would spend it with other students of similar age while the parents would meet in my living room. When I suggested to Mrs. Oliver that she might enjoy talking with other parents, she revealed something most remarkable. She said, "That would be fantastic. Every day I pick up my daughter from school. I see many other parents running in the school to pick up their own children. We recognize each other, but we've never said more than hello after many months. It would be so great to sit down and have a conversation with another parent."

Through parent-peer conversations, parents share meaningful, hands-on experience. They take stock of the conflicts and celebrations, problems and solutions that are part of daily life. Furthermore, and perhaps more importantly, when parents talk about their parenting experiences with each other, they give voice to their own sense of self. When parents share the sometimes chaotic and improbable details of their parenting experiences with each other, they intuitively hear themselves in each other's stories. They recognize their own voices in the commonality of shared parental experience. Of course, there are other resources that parents can seek out, such as teachers and extended family members. However, because parent-peers operate "in the trenches," actively participating in the daily challenges and pleasures of raising children, peer relationships support and empower parents' deeply rooted sense of self in ways that only other parents can provide.

TEACHERS LETTING GO

From MBT's Studio

It's the end of August and I'm calling all my students to organize the upcoming schedule. When Mrs. Fuhrman informs me that over the summer, they decided to switch teachers, I am more than slightly taken aback. I was under the impression that everything was going well. There was no indication at the end of the previous term that anything was amiss. I feel awkward and ill-prepared for how to respond.

On many occasions during my career, I have assisted students with switching to other teachers, in particular when I thought another teacher could better meet the needs of particular students. So, when parents like Mrs. Fuhrman inform me (at what I consider to be the very last minute) of their plans to switch teachers, I'll admit to feeling a variety of emotions—disappointment, annoyance, frustration, helplessness—followed by periods of doubt during which I seriously question the quality of my teaching. I wonder if perhaps there really is something wrong with my teaching approach.

While this has only occurred on a small number of unanticipated occasions, I have found the situation to be concerning. Sometimes, as in Mrs. Fuhrman's case, it arrived at the beginning of a term when I had already put aside time in my schedule for the student. Most disconcerting were the occasions when, in the middle of a term, parents informed me. Such unanticipated events seemed out of place given the preceding months or years of what I thought was effective communication. What I've come to understand and accept is that parents and teachers may differ in how they interpret taking action in the "best interest" of the child. Parents can switch their children to another teacher without any input from their current teacher. While the current teacher's connection with other music colleagues and their knowledge of the child may be useful, parents can choose to go their own route however ill-advised or well-informed that may be. Parents are the designated decision makers for their children, which means that "letting go" of uncomfortable situations has become a necessary part of my teaching approach. It's not in any teacher's best interest to admonish their teaching approach or become obsessive about trying to figure out what could have been done differently. I'm not saying that "letting go" is easy to do, however, when parents bring an end to further interaction, the best thing teachers can do is to move on.

Teaching Tip

√ Let go of uncomfortable circumstances
beyond your area of influence.

1. Set a reasonable time period for reflection.
2. Reach out to colleagues for support
and advice where appropriate.
3. Acknowledge the limitations of what you may accomplish.

In a similar vein, a colleague told me about an event called "Dealing with Difficult Parents," which was hosted by a local music teachers group. It was another reminder that teachers can face less than optimal situations when working with parents. During my forty-year piano teaching career, I've come to learn that a family's home life is well beyond my area of influence. Regrettably, I have witnessed children subjected to shame and fear from their parents. While my immediate reaction was to be the protective shield for my students, my efforts were largely unsuccessful. In cases where parents had an obsessive control over their child, they responded to my suggestions of stepping back by switching to a teacher less concerned about parents' actions. Such occurrences echo the sentiments of colleagues who routinely relate stories of how things have backfired with parental involvement. I'm thankful that negative interactions are the exception and not the rule.

Your Thoughts

Uncomfortable circumstances may catch teachers off guard.

1. What kinds of uncomfortable circumstances seem to be unavoidable in music teaching?
2. Which colleagues may you reach out to for support?

Chapter 4

OPENING DOORS

As a child who studied traditional piano, I attended every single piano lesson on my own. During that time, I have scant memories of my parents ever talking with my piano teachers. They had obligatory rushed conversations following performances, but other than that, it seemed my parents had little connection to my instructors. Prior to pivotal experiences in 1980 with an Australian family and the colleague with whom I shared my teaching studio, it never occurred to me how I would involve parents in their child's musical development or what would be the outstanding benefits.

Knowing that music teaching strategies must connect meaningfully with students' family home musical life, what stands out for me is how working with parents isn't just about teachers telling parents what to do. It's about respecting and accepting parents as real-life individuals whose participation includes a wealth of experience and the unavoidable obstacles of daily living they encounter. Under such circumstances, it involves valuing parents for who they are and what they're prepared to do, rather than trying to reconfigure them into some kind of cookie-cutter format or idyllic version of parental involvement. It's important for me to be the teacher parents can depend on—a teacher not bound by precast models or inflexible teaching regimes.

When possible, I open doors for parents, introduce them to meaningful ways of thinking about teaching and learning, and connect them with peers. It's my responsibility to make personal connections with parents' ideologies, attitudes, and philosophies and to link with the expansive resource of what parents already know about life. Accepting parents as real-life individuals is a liberating experience because how they participate in their child's musical development is based on their own lives, priorities, and background—not mine—even though we may share innumerable commonalities. The goal is to welcome students into richly satisfying and joyful journeys of learning to sing or play a musical instrument with the intention of building on and exercising the family home life that's already there.

FAQs

Q: I have run into the obstacle of parents requesting lessons for a month to see if their child likes it before they make a commitment. I thought it would better if they made a one-year commitment, as progress can be fairly slow at the beginning. Is there anything I can do to get parents to change their minds?

A: This question is compelling because it speaks to two fundamental aspects of teaching and learning: mutual trust among teachers, students, and parents and parents' concern over their child's engagement. It reminds me of a colleague who put mutual trust and student engagement at the forefront by teaching the student's first lesson at no cost. He teaches the first lesson for free, knowing he can make it so interesting, engaging, fun, rewarding, personal, and successful that of course students would want to come back for more. His message is clear: that he appreciates students' willingness to explore with him, that he knows how to engage them, and that he's got the tools to make things work. As demonstrative of trustworthy and engaging music lessons, I think it's a brilliant strategy!

When I learned of my colleague's strategy, I must admit it gave me food for thought. While I don't teach the first lesson for free, my strategy for new students takes into consideration mutual trust and parents' concern over their child's reaction. My solution is to start with a six-week lesson period during which I give my best efforts to make lessons so engaging and successful that students eagerly continue. I make a point to frequently highlight evidence of progress that might go unnoticed by students and parents, given their inexperience with music lessons. Most notably, I have students give a concert from their first lesson onward and encourage them to do the same when they get home. When possible, I connect parents with each other as well as students.

I trust that students and parents also give their best efforts to six weeks of lessons. This period is generally enough time for teacher, student, and parents to get an idea of how things will proceed. As teacher, I can see what kind of progress the student has made and get a sense of how I'll help make it work for them given the obstacles they may face. Students and parents get an idea of what's involved in taking music lessons and how it fits in with their family's home life. Most often at the end of the six weeks, students and parents choose to continue with lessons. Therefore, this strategy is useful in establishing a trustworthy and engaging instructional process. It's also a practical approach when obstacles make it difficult for successful continuation, as students and parents can opt out after six weeks.

Q: Many parents in my studio seem to take practicing as a serious activity for their children. What about making room for "playfulness" in music studies?

A: There is more than ample room for playfulness in music studies. Parents are seasoned experts when it comes to playfulness in their child's upbringing. They know how to play peekaboo, make up stories, throw a ball just for fun. And they may easily forget about playfulness in their efforts to help their child achieve musical success. They may think it's quicker if they just get down to business and work as hard as possible.

Something to keep in mind is that adults and children interpret play in different ways. Typically, adults think of play as an activity bounded by a framework of rules, like the game of soccer. Each player knows the rules of the game and abides by them. For children, play is more about how the game evolves as it proceeds. A game may end up with a different structure than it began with—a dragon may turn into a flower, a girl may become a superhero, a tragic ending may have a silver lining. Spontaneity in play allows children to experiment with different social roles such as being the leader or teacher. Make-believe and imaginary play encourage creativity and build communication and language skills—a challenge may require a magical solution; an instrument becomes an entire landscape. Children's explanations can reveal a lot about what they understand. They can make up words for songs or tasks.

What's key is that children need to feel free enough to play but also safe enough to engage in play and reap its benefits. This means parents may need to become adept at both setting the stage for play and getting out of the way so their child's imaginative approach leads the way.

Build On and Exercise What's Already There

Part 1: Working with parents is about respecting and accepting them as real-life individuals.

1. Choose two or three student-family home contexts in your studio.

2. Describe what you know about students' family home life.

3. How do you currently build on and exercise what's already there?

4. What could you do differently?

NOTES

1. Benedict Carey, *How We Learn: The Surprising Truth About When, Where, and Why It Happens* (New York: Random House, 2015).

2. Peter Brown, Henry Rodiger, and Mark McDaniel, *Make It Stick: The Science of Successful Learning* (Cambridge, MA: Harvard University Press, 2014).

3. Andrea Creech, "The Role of the Family in Supporting Learning," in *The Oxford Handbook of Music Psychology*, edited by S. Hallam and I. T. Cross (Oxford, UK: Oxford University Press, 2009), 295–306.

4. John Dewey, *How We Think* (Boston, MA: Houghton Mifflin, 1933).

5. Leon Festinger, *A Theory of Cognitive Dissonance* (Stanford, CA: Stanford University Press, 1957).

6. Daniel Berlyne, "A Theory of Human Curiosity," *British Journal of Psychology* 45 no. 3 (1954): 180–91.

7. G. McPherson and J. Davidson, "Playing an Instrument," in *The Child as Musician* edited by G. McPherson (Oxford, UK: Oxford University Press, 2006), 331–51.

8. Creech, "The Role of the Family in Supporting Learning," 295–306.

9. L. Iscoe and K. Bordelon, "Parents: Peer Support for Parents of Handicapped Children," *Children's Health Care* 14 no. 2 (1985): 103–9.

10. M. Bell, R. Fitzgerald, and M. Legge, "Parent Peer Advocacy, Information and Refusing Disability Discourses," *New Zealand Journal of Social Sciences Online* 8 no. 1–2 (2013): 1–12.

Part 2

PRACTICING

Music gives spark to the flame
that is the individual's sense of self.

No matter the level of musicianship
amateur or professional, casual or dedicated,
music ignites something deep inside every person.

No matter how much time
we spend at the instrument,
no matter how difficult the repertoire,
no matter finishing the piece,
we go back for more because
music reminds us of who we are.

Chapter 5

Framework of Basic Human Needs

Today, there's no shortage of resources on the topic of practicing. Just type "practicing a musical instrument" into a quick Google search and you'll find "Top 10 Practicing Tips," "Practice Like an Expert," "Efficient Practice," or "Organizing Your Practice." While these resources share similarities in the way they standardize practicing so that anyone can be successful, I feel they're not entirely adequate because they don't take into consideration what compels a person to practice. Of course, people practice musical instruments and singing because of their connection to music, because of the irresistible pull that music exerts on many people. That's probably the most obvious motive for compelling people to practice.

What may not be so obvious is how practicing fulfills the need that many individuals have to validate their sense of self and their desire for experiencing a coherent sense of self. Researchers Edward Deci and Richard Ryan describe it as achieving a sense of personal wholeness, vitality, and integrity wherein individuals tend naturally to seek challenges, discover new perspectives, stretch their capacities, and express their propensities in order to actualize their human potentials.[1] Practicing is just one of many activities that acts as an affirmation of who we are and what we do. It's more than just following a teacher's instructions. Practicing satisfies five basic human needs that are linked to people's sense of self and important to the experiences of their everyday lives. These five needs offer a personal framework for the way we approach life, for the strategies we use to maintain positive health, growth, and attitude in our lives. They are as follows:

- Autonomy: The need to feel that our personal efforts or pursuits are internally generated and implemented rather than externally influenced or imposed. The need to direct our own lives.

- Fluency: The need to feel personally effective/successful in acquiring competency and executing skills necessary to our pursuits. The need for mastery of aspects in our own lives.
- Purpose: The need to feel that our personal efforts or pursuits are meaningful. The need to create things that are vital for our own lives.
- Relatedness: The need to feel that our personal efforts or pursuits are connected and relevant to the surrounding social context. The need to participate in our world.
- Reflection: The need to consider how our personal efforts or pursuits contribute to and detract from our own lives. The need to critically question and examine our personal efforts and pursuits.

These needs play key roles in the infinite number of personal activities that make us feel secure, capable, vital, and socially integrated. Knowing about them explains a lot about practicing. When practicing doesn't fulfill any of these five basic needs, we most likely will not pursue it. We may find practicing boring or worthless. Conversely, when practicing responds to our basic needs or combinations thereof, our involvement takes on a self-sustained momentum and energy that we can't get enough of. We experience practicing as something worthwhile and compelling, something that's essential to our own lives, our sense of self, our character, our identity.

Part 2 explores these five basic human needs as the practical and inspirational framework for practicing. In chapters 6 through 10, I consider autonomy, fluency, purpose, relatedness, and reflection in the real-life setting of teaching music students. In chapter 11, I incorporate an additional, and especially important, aspect related to vocal and instrumental practicing—listening—our need to transform the sounds in our heads into the sounds we make in performance. Listening has implications regarding students' current repertoire study, their future practicing, as well as making social connections.

The framework of the five basic human needs comes from three primary research resources. First, from the University of Rochester, Professors Edward Deci and Richard Ryan summarize their research into human development and growth in their 2002 benchmark resource *Handbook of Self-Determination Research*.[2] Deci and Ryan identify competence, relatedness, and autonomy as three cornerstones of their understanding of self-determination. The impact of Deci and Ryan's research is far-reaching in addressing theory as well as potential applications ranging from parenting and education to business management and sports.

Second, from author and social analyst Daniel Pink. Working from Deci and Ryan's research into self-determination theory, Pink maintains Deci and Ryan's focus on autonomy and mastery and brings in an additional aspect:

the importance of purpose. With organizations, business, parents, and educators as his target audiences, Pink's book *Drive*[3] makes a convincing case that autonomy, mastery, and purpose are the secret to performance and satisfaction at work, school, and at home.

Third, from music education researcher Gary McPherson and colleagues. Following a research project that spanned fourteen years and closely followed the lives of more than 150 children learning music, this research team identified competence, relatedness, and autonomy as important factors in students' primary and secondary school musical experiences. Published in 2012, *Music In Our Lives*,[4] provides the framework and theory for further investigation and discussion in the field of music education.

Finally, in addition to this combination of autonomy, fluency/competency, purpose, and relatedness, I felt it was essential to include reflection as necessary to determining what's working and what's not working in learning processes. I take inspiration from Arthur Costa and Bena Kallick's research[5] into metacognition (thinking about thinking) as well as Adam Grant's *Think Again*.[6] My goal in part 2 is to build on the work of the above researchers and to explore the framework of five basic human needs in the context of music studio teaching.

Please note that I treat the terms "autonomy" and "independence" as synonyms. Previously, in part 1, I employed the expression "independence and ownership" in keeping with parental attitudes toward child independence. In part 2, I continue with the term "autonomy" in keeping with the language employed consistently among the sources of Deci and Ryan, Pink, and McPherson and colleagues.

Your Thoughts

Autonomy, fluency, purpose, relatedness, reflection, and listening play key roles in shaping how musicians practice.

1. Which of the above seem the most familiar? Why?
2. Which of the above would you like to know more about?

NOTES

1. Edward Deci and Richard Ryan, *Handbook of Self-determination Research* (Rochester, NY: University of Rochester Press, 2002).
2. Ibid.

3. Daniel Pink, *Drive: The Surprising Truth about What Motivates Us* (New York: Riverhead Books, 2009).

4. G. E. McPherson, J. W. Davidson, and R. Faulkner, *Music in Our Lives* (Oxford, UK: Oxford University Press, 2012).

5. Arthur Costa and Bena Kallick, *Learning and Leading with Habits of Mind* (Alexandria, VA: ASCD, 2008).

6. Adam Grant, *Think Again* (New York: Viking, 2021).

Chapter 6

Practicing and Autonomy

Autonomy is the need to feel that our personal efforts or pursuits are internally generated and implemented rather than externally imposed or determined. It's the need to direct our own lives.

From MBT's Studio

Six months of lessons meant five-year-old Sean could play several pieces. One week, the moment his older sister finished her lesson, Sean climbed quickly onto the bench. "Watch this!" he exclaimed and launched, without hesitation, into a boisterous performance of his newest piece. It was like watching a locomotive barreling its way across an open landscape with determination as its destination.

Connie is fifteen years old and studying at the senior level. During one lesson, something about the look on her face told me that she had questions. She placed her score on the music stand and looked hopefully in my direction, in a kind of wishful anticipation that I would somehow intuitively figure out what she needed. "How are things going?" I asked. "Mmm . . . " Connie began with uncertainty. "I just don't know. There's so much to work on," she continued. "I hear you," I replied. "Where shall we start?"

I begin this chapter with Sean and Connie because their stories illustrate how autonomy looks different from one student to the next; how practicing takes on differing characteristics from one student to another. Autonomy in Sean's case resonates with his boundless enthusiasm for taking risks, attempting his best shot without being held back by the fear of failure or the disappointment associated with making mistakes. In contrast, Connie's autonomy is concerned with safety and certainty, with accessing information that may dispel doubt or indecision. My responsibility as their teacher is to support each student's own autonomous attempts to take charge of their practicing.

Your Thoughts

1. Which of your students resemble Sean? What do they need from you?
2. Which of your students resemble Connie? How do you help them?

As an aspect of practicing, autonomy is about a person's basic need to feel in charge of their own activities or pursuits. Autonomy is synonymous with notions of independence and freedom, especially as it relates to a person's feelings, thoughts, and actions. Autonomy is something we acknowledge as an unavoidable and necessary element of children's growth. From the two-year-old child's penchant for the word "No," along with their irrepressible drive to do things their own way, to the sulking and rebellious teenager's inherent need to separate oneself from family and eventually from peers, these are the inevitable signs of child independence. Autonomy is also something we admire in an adult's ability to figure things out and make decisions.

For University of Rochester researchers Edward Deci and Richard Ryan, autonomy is important because of the value we place on acting from our own interests and integrated values. Autonomous individuals experience their behavior as an expression of the self. Working autonomously has been linked to creativity and innovation, particularly in the work of Harvard graduate and author Susan Cain, who asserts that the current emphasis on groupthink (i.e., working in teams) may actually "stifle productivity at work and deprive schoolchildren of the skills they'll need to achieve excellence in an increasingly competitive world."[1] Autonomy can be a powerful catalyst for personal achievement and innovation. It deserves attention from employers in setting up working environments and for teachers in creating educational circumstances that foster meaningful student growth. Daniel Pink describes autonomy in terms of the deeply-rooted need to direct our own lives, as the launchpad that propels us to learn and create new things, to do better by ourselves and our world.[2]

Given the recognized value of autonomy across all stages of life, I find it intriguing when I meet teachers who aren't entirely comfortable with the notion of student autonomy, teachers who actively discourage autonomy as an element of practicing. So, before I pursue any further examination into autonomy, it seems prudent to respond to the question, "What makes teachers uncomfortable with student autonomy?"

ASSUMPTIONS ABOUT AUTONOMY

One of teachers' most common assumptions about autonomy is that by the time autonomous students seek guidance from them, students may have taken on all sorts of undesirable directions. Teachers assume that once students' musical directions are set in place, teachers will be hard-pressed, if not incapable, of guiding, modifying, or making adjustments. The only way to prevent students from taking undesirable directions in the first place is for teachers to always maintain strict control over their students' development.

Your Thoughts

Autonomy refers to our need to feel that we're in charge of what we do and how we choose to achieve it.

1. How do you feel about autonomy? For yourself? For your students?
2. What do you think about the risk of autonomous students acquiring "bad habits"?

In her book *How Popular Musicians Learn*, music education scholar Lucy Green makes a noteworthy argument related to teachers' fear of student autonomy. Green interviewed popular musicians regarding their experience with converting their self-developed techniques to established techniques derived from classical music instruction. Her research reveals that popular musicians found it easy to adopt new aspects of technique even after years without the specialized guidance of an experienced teacher or performer. Green concludes that popular musicians are able to adopt radical changes to their performance habits because they maintain a more flexible and less emotionally alienating approach to music learning.[3] Because they autonomously develop musical habits on the basis of volunteerism and enjoyment as compared to being under a teacher's control, these musicians feel very much at ease in adjusting their performance approach.

This example is remarkable in the way it demonstrates how autonomy isn't some kind of self-centered extremism that makes people immune to what others might have to say or paralyses them into permanent inflexibility. Being autonomous is more of an underlying perspective that influences people in their attempts to become aware of, identify, interrogate, or evaluate the strategies they use to pursue their lives. It differs immensely from the close-minded, go-it-alone, listen-to-nobody-else mentality that teachers may fear in autonomous students. Rather, autonomy functions much like an astute internal feedback system that lets each of us know whether or not we've actually taken charge of what we're doing with our own lives.

Students' sense of autonomy has a powerful effect on their thoughts, feelings, and actions in practicing a musical instrument. In my studio, I've witnessed how consistently incorporating my students' autonomy has resulted in them taking great satisfaction with their own efforts and coming up with practical ideas and inspiration beyond my own experience. With autonomy as our common grounding for musical exploration, I'm always fascinated by the topics my students bring to their lessons. For example:

From MBT's Studio

Thirteen-year-old Keenan began his lesson with a fledgling existential question, "Why are we here?" I responded, "Well, I think we can probably come up with at least three reasons. Why don't you go first?" I wasn't the least bit surprised when Keenan put "Creativity" at the top of his list before the two of us collaboratively brought a couple more answers to his inquiry.

Looking back on our brief philosophical conversation, several factors related to Keenan's autonomy stand out. First, he felt secure enough in our relationship to make an inquiry into the point of music lessons. Second, I invited Keenan to share his own insight before contributing my own thoughts. And third, from an alternate perspective, I could have said we don't have time for such questions or given him my authoritative view on the matter and cut short such a conversation. However, by being open to Keenan's already percolating inquiry and encouraging him to voice his own thoughts, I confirmed how much I value him as an autonomous human being. Keenan can trust that he doesn't need to silence his thoughts just because he's having a piano lesson. Music lessons aren't isolated from the rest of life; they're a continuation of what's going on in his life.

LANGUAGE AND GESTURES

Generally speaking, I don't recall having many existential conversations with my students over the past four decades of teaching. However, I do remember a specific event that was pivotal in bringing my attention to the language and gestures supportive of students' autonomy. During the late 1970s, at the suggestion of a colleague, I read a marvelous book by Dorothy Corkille Briggs that would permanently impact my instructional approach—*Your Child's Self-Esteem: The Key to Life.* Based on twenty-five years of working with parents and children, Briggs synthesizes her experiences as mother, psychologist, and teacher to look at child development from a new perspective. Her goal is to provide a cohesive framework that positions children's growth and behavior against the backdrop of their search for identity and respect. Children, she says, value themselves to the degree that they have been valued. The body language, tones of voice, and facial expressions of those around them send children an ongoing stream of messages. Words also play an immensely influential role, Briggs emphasizes. "There's no question about it; words have power. They can shred or build self-respect."[4] Nearly four decades later, I still recall how Briggs's convincing narrative affected my approach as a novice teacher. At the time, I could see exactly what Briggs was talking about in my own teaching and in my observations of other teachers.

Your Thoughts

Take a moment to consider your teaching language and gestures.

1. What stands out?
2. What messages do you think your language and gestures convey to your students? Competency? Dependence? Collaboration? Creativity? Other?

As teachers, we convey messages through our words and actions that sometimes support students' autonomy and at other times leave it completely out of the picture. In the years since reading Briggs's convincing account, I've made some deliberate choices about my instructional language and gestures to reinforce my students as autonomous musicians.[5] The following scenarios illustrate what I mean.

Scenario 1: The clarinet student arrives for their lesson. The teacher assembles the student's clarinet and hands it to the student before retrieving the notebook, musical scores, and other lesson materials from the student.

Scenario 2: The clarinet student arrives for their lesson. The student assembles their clarinet and tests it out before handing the notebook, musical scores, and other lesson materials to the teacher.

From a teacher proficiency perspective, it may seem appropriate for the teacher in Scenario 1 to take charge of gestures like assembling the clarinet. After all, they can do it more quickly and precisely than students, therein saving precious time, eliminating student inaccuracy, and increasing overall efficiency. However, from a student autonomy perspective, Scenario 1 teacher's gestures indirectly convey a message that the student is less capable and less efficient compared to the teacher. Starting the lesson with students taking charge in Scenario 2 sets up a clear message that the teacher has confidence in the student's decision-making. They believe in students' autonomy. Such simple gestures provide students with opportunities to demonstrate their understanding as well as their willingness to be responsible and accountable. Moreover, when students are unsure or unsuccessful in their attempts, such occasions serve as opportunities for clarinet teacher and student to revisit the assembly process.

Teaching Tip

√ Actions speak volumes. Teachers' and students' gestures reveal a lot about who's in charge.

1. Empower students' ownership of their own musical journey.
2. Respond to inaccuracies with discussion and demonstration.

Scenario 3: Before the violin student performs a junior-level piece, the teacher says, "I want you to pay close attention to your dynamics and steady beat now that you've been working on them the entire week." Student performs. Teacher responds, "I see you got your dynamics on page 1, but pages 2 and 3 still need work and so does the beat."

Scenario 4: Before the violin student performs a junior-level piece, the teacher says, "Tell me, what were you working on in this piece last week?" Student replies, "Beat and dynamics." Teacher continues, "Great! I'm curious to see how it turns out." Student performs. Teacher responds, "Tell me what you noticed about your beat and dynamics." Student replies, "Some good, some bad."

Once again, from a teacher proficiency perspective, it may seem appropriate for the teacher in Scenario 3 to provide efficient directions that immediately steer the student to the task at hand. Unfortunately, such strategies have the potential to turn students into passive consumers of lesson time. While putting the student in charge in Scenario 4 may be more time-consuming, this process allows the teacher to not only gain useful information but also to get a sense of the student's mindset. Through this exchange, the teacher puts together a picture of what went on at home and recognizes the student as an autonomous individual capable of directing their own positive development—no matter how novice or experienced that may be.

Teaching Tip

√ Watch your language. Words have the power
to either fuel or deny students' autonomy.

1. Nurture students as thinking and communicative individuals.
2. Encourage students' communication
skills in age-appropriate ways.
3. Be patient.

WHAT ABOUT MISTAKES?

Scenario 5: An advanced guitar student performs a selection from memory. When the performance is complete, the teacher opens the musical score to the appropriate page and places it in front of the student. The teacher takes a pencil and marks the score while saying, "You have these wrong notes." The teacher performs the designated bars with the correct notes before saying, "Make sure you fix the wrong notes this week."

Scenario 6: An advanced guitar student performs a selection from memory. When the performance is complete, the teacher asks the student to open their musical score to the appropriate page. The teacher asks the student to point to the bars with wrong notes. The teacher gives a pencil to the student and asks, "Do you need help writing in the notes or the fingerings?" The student confirms as appropriate. The teacher continues by validating the student's contribution or providing information while the student writes in the score. The teacher asks the student to perform the designated bars with the correct notes and wrong notes before saying, "Why not make sure you can play both the right and wrong notes this week."

At first glance, it may appear as if the teacher in Scenario 5 has been generous by fast-forwarding through marking the score and giving the student autonomous responsibility over fixing the wrong notes. There's merit in this approach. There's also a disadvantage. Language and gestures such as these remove students from the process of identifying, clarifying, and resolving issues related to performance development. That's where the teacher in Scenario 6 succeeds by allowing the student to take the lead in resolving mistakes and providing guidance that fosters the student's autonomy. The dangers in Scenario 5 are that students may fail to follow-through because they're not engaged in the learning process, or they fix their mistakes out of passive obligation to their teacher. In Scenario 6, students benefit by actively taking control of their own mistakes and solutions for themselves. As pianist William

Westney suggests in his book *The Perfect Wrong Note*, playing a wrong note can be constructive, useful, even enlightening and teachers play a key role in helping students develop trust and awareness in their own development.⁶ One thing I know well is that students frequently dislike teachers telling them about mistakes they're already aware of. As a consequence, I purposefully support students' autonomy by building on their awareness and helping them implement successful solutions to resolving mistakes.

Teaching Tip

√ Mistakes aren't the problem. Mistakes are part of the solution.

1. Empower students to identify mistakes.
2. Empower students to clarify both mistakes and what's correct.
3. Empower students to resolve mistakes.
4. Be patient.

Teachers may ask, "What if students aren't aware of any mistakes in their performance?" I can honestly say that in nearly four decades of teaching, I've rarely met a student who couldn't point out their own mistakes. However, when students are unaware of things going wrong, I'm responsible for alerting them without excluding their autonomy or disrespecting their participation. In most cases, I start by saying something like, "I can see why you might not have noticed what's going wrong in this section," before I hand them a pencil. No matter their age or penmanship skills, giving them responsibility for marking the score has several advantages: adding visual reminders to the score, using writing to engage students as a distinct aspect of learning, and involving students as active participants. Furthermore, it helps to get students accustomed to marking their scores as an intentional precursor to their accurate performance.

PROTECTING STUDENTS

From MBT's Studio

It's two days before the year-end concert. At her lesson, sixteen-year-old advanced student Maya reveals she's had a busy week at school with three departmental exams. Unfortunately, she hasn't practiced at all since her last lesson. For the concert, she is scheduled to play two selections: a three-page technically-easy selection by Rameau and a six-page technically-advanced selection by Chopin. She starts with a successful performance of the Rameau. Then, as she performs the Chopin, it falls apart from beginning to end. Before I can say anything, Maya hurriedly suggests, "I have all day Saturday to practice it. I am sure I can get it ready." I continue, "I hear where you're coming from and thanks so much for offering, but I don't think one day of crammed practice is a healthy choice. It's not the same as cramming for an exam. I'm sorry to say we'll need to wait for another opportunity to perform the Chopin."

Sound familiar? Have you ever had a student who thought cramming for a concert was a positive strategy? What about other ways students may unintentionally bring harm to their musical skill set? One of the responsibilities I take seriously is protecting my students from harmful practicing strategies. I understand that students' limited experience with piano performance may not equip them with the knowledge to see how easily they may damage their own performance skill set. Fortunately, there is a great deal of published material available for music teachers that addresses vocal and instrumental injury prevention.[7]

All music teachers face challenges related to the potential for irreversible damage in their students. I've met highly motivated, autonomous students who suffered a variety of injuries. A French horn player who damaged her embouchure. A cellist who couldn't play for a year due to an arm injury. A pianist whose tendonitis resulted in withdrawing from music lessons. A vocalist who strained his voice by practicing well beyond the point of exhaustion. It seems there is no end to the ways students may be affected by injury.

Teaching Tip

√ Protect students from harmful practice strategies.

1. Practicing isn't like cramming for an exam.
2. There are limits on students' emotional and physical capacities.

When Maya indicates she's willing to cram a week's worth of consistent practice into one day, her suggestion sets off alarm bells for me. On the one hand, I admire her autonomy and confidence. She's achieved an advanced level of performance through dedication and hard work. Yet on the other hand, her youthful experience does not provide her with a view of long-term outcomes. Of course, she's disappointed not to perform the Chopin at the year-end concert. Therefore, I need to ensure she understands that I'm well aware of her feelings. Her disappointment is real to me.

Unfortunately, processes that result in injuries to students' musical skill set may be difficult for them to identify because, in the moment, students may not know what to look for. The seeds of injury may seem inconsequential or not worth paying attention to. For students like Maya, I want to help her understand that we all have limits on our emotional and physical capacities. This means I regularly have open conversations with Maya about healthy and sustainable routines that give her the opportunity to expand her awareness and take charge of her evolving development. My goal is to help Maya take care of herself so that she may enjoy many years of satisfying, injury-free musical exploration.

HOMEWORK NOTES

Scenario 7: At lesson's end, the teacher writes out the trumpet student's homework in a notebook, including pertinent information regarding the various bars and specific elements to work on in each piece. The teacher gives the notebook to the student to assist with their home practice.

Scenario 8: At lesson's end, the teacher writes out the trumpet student's homework in a notebook. For the first piece, the teacher asks, "Can you look in the score and tell me which bars need help?" Similarly for other pieces, the teacher asks, "What needs extra attention in this piece? Is it the phrasing or articulation?" For each piece, the student responds appropriately, or the teacher assists the student to recall important elements to work on. The teacher gives the notebook to the student to assist with their home practice.

From a perspective of student autonomy, it may seem as if both Scenario 7 and 8 miss a major consideration—autonomous students should make their own notes, not their teachers. The problem, especially at the beginner or elementary level, is that the amount of teacher's input necessary for making meaningful notes would most likely overshadow a student's autonomy. It makes sense for teachers to make notes (or dictate notes to the parent as described in chapter 3), while keeping in mind the importance of actively involving students in the process. I've found that including my students in this final activity allows both of us to revisit the lesson's various aspects, to see whether or not we were both on the same page, and identify where certain activities might have resulted in students coming away with a completely different conclusion.

When students take notes (as my eight-year-olds and older students did throughout the 2020–2021 pandemic), in addition to my own instructions, I might say something like, "What should you write in your notebook?" or

"Which bar needs fingering help?" or "What challenge do you want with this piece?" Every online lesson begins with an equipment check to make sure pencil, notebook, and repertoire materials are ready to go.

Teaching Tip

√ Taking homework notes is a shared, collaborative process.

1. Get confirmation of students' ownership verbally or through demonstration.
2. Revisit homework points during the lesson period and at its conclusion.
3. Provide meaningful follow-up at the next lesson.

TEACHER'S BELIEF IN AUTONOMY

Some teachers mistakenly think that student autonomy refers to students teaching themselves and that they have no need for their teachers. As the above scenarios demonstrate, student autonomy doesn't mean teachers are pushed out of the picture. It means teachers use language and gestures that foster students' active participation. Autonomous students depend on teachers to create and maintain supportive learning environments so students may take charge of and be actively involved in their own learning.

What stands out for me in this exploration is that teachers genuinely incorporate student autonomy in their teaching, not just because it appears in an educational resource that highlights the top ten teaching tips. Teachers are attentive to student autonomy because it matters to them, because they cannot imagine what their teaching would look like without it. Teachers recognize that autonomy, like most other aspects of human nature, comes with its own benefits and drawbacks. When a student like Sean shows up with his newest piece, or Connie comes with insecurities, or Keenan questions the meaning of music lessons, or Maya suggests cramming for a concert, teachers recognize that autonomous students depend on their teachers for guidance. This means teachers do their best to respond with honest feedback and unconditional respect that builds on students' autonomy and fills in the gaps as needed.

FAQs

Q: In principle, I like the idea of students' autonomy. But what do you do when students' autonomy results in them choosing repertoire that's well beyond their current level of mastery? Isn't that just asking for trouble?

A: Many years ago, I had a conversation with a colleague that completely transformed my comfort with students choosing their own repertoire. They used a 50/50 approach—choosing 50 percent of students' repertoire and students choosing the other 50 percent—explaining that when students really want to learn a piece, there's absolutely nothing teachers can do to stop them. And why would teachers want to stop students from learning on their own? Isn't the whole point of music studies to develop students' music learning skills so they can be successful without their teacher?

In addition to my appreciation for the motivation behind students' own choice, what I've also noticed in applying my colleague's 50/50 approach is that students gradually become familiar with their own set of learning skills. Beginners rely on their ability to play by ear. Elementary reading students find sources on the internet that offer easy arrangements of their favorite pieces. Junior to advanced students explore what's necessary to make pop song arrangements playable and sound like the original recording. Senior classical students find out that not all repertoire suits their personality or fits under their hands—similar to the way we imagine that Elton John and Lang Lang tailor their performances to synchronize with their personal passion, technical competency, and audience interest.

For students in my studio who may be hesitant about making their initial choices, the annual Student Choice Concert is a great way for them to see the variety of choices other students are making. When students choose repertoire well beyond their learning mastery, I'm always open to see how far they can get. Sometimes they get further than I anticipated. With my help, they may acquire more manageable processes that are outside their own experiences. On other occasions, there's nothing wrong with moving on after initial efforts prove unsuccessful.

Q: Recently, I observed a master voice teacher teaching master class lessons. At first, I couldn't understand why the teacher taught every student with a different approach. I soon realized that the teacher tailored each lesson to the individual student's autonomy. My question is how can teachers possibly get a sense of the student's autonomy in such a brief amount of time?

A: Thank you for noticing how the master teacher adapted their approach to synchronize with each student's sense of self. Watching experienced teachers in action can be challenging because they make their teaching look deceptively easy and natural, when most likely their ease and naturalness results from many years of trial and error. The first step toward greater confidence with your own teaching ability is to jump in and try things out.

In my own teaching, I frequently rely on my intuition. I trust my first impressions to guide my actions. I pay attention to students' tone of voice, eye contact, performance gestures, choice of words, body language, breathing or lack thereof, pacing, and where they look. When my intuitive snapshots turn out to be accurate, on we go with Plan A. When they turn out to be inaccurate, I waste no time in gathering more information. Sometimes I ask questions, other times I make statements. Either way, I'm looking for confirmation of what I think might work for Plan B. When needed, I move to Plan C and D.

Generally speaking, I've noticed that everyone has the capacity for intuitive awareness. For example, we can intuitively tell when someone is feeling unwell or distressed. We can intuit whether a person is laidback or uptight upon first meeting. We can get a sense of whether we're compatible with someone or not at a social gathering. Similarly, teachers can quickly put together an intuitive snapshot of students. Getting comfortable with using your intuition is a great starting point. Just remember to keep refining your picture with more information as you move along.

Q: I think I get where you're going with the emphasis on students' autonomy. That students appreciate being able to take charge of their own efforts. My question is how can you possibly get autonomy to happen in the very first lesson? Isn't it something that students eventually achieve rather than something they start with?

A: What I always like to keep in mind is that when students begin music lessons, they already have a vast array of autonomous experiences. They can dress and feed themselves. They can make decisions about what TV shows they want to watch, what video games they want to play. They may have an uncanny expertise with computer technology. From the very first lesson, I most assuredly want to keep contributing to students' autonomy. My preferred strategy to ensure students' autonomy is to conclude their very first lesson with their own concert performance. I want students to experience their musical expertise (no matter how limited) as something to celebrate and share with others. Of course, I'm interested in students developing musical excellence, but I have lots of time to attend to musical excellence in the weeks and months ahead.

What does a first lesson concert look like? It includes three steps: bow to the audience, performance, bow to the audience. I demonstrate how bowing to the audience before our performance is how we let the audience know we're ready to begin. Bowing after is our way of letting the audience know we've finished, and they may applaud enthusiastically. Depending on students' age and readiness, my piano students may perform any of the activities we explored during their lesson. For example, play a five-finger exercise, play a rhythmic excerpt (peanut butter sandwich) with one finger, clap a rhythmic excerpt. The point is to make it short and easy. Encouraging students to give concert performances in their own homes is an excellent strategy to ensure they receive ongoing recognition for the autonomous journey that's well underway.

Q: I spend a lot of time demonstrating and explaining to students how to make improvements to their musicianship. However, I'm not sure why everything has often disappeared when they return the next week. How can teachers be certain their students actually have ownership of details that occur during the lesson?

A: You are absolutely on the right track with demonstrating and explaining how students may take ownership of details. These are two excellent teaching tools. What I find challenging is that what's obvious for me may not be obvious for my students. Demonstrations and explanations, which make complete sense to me, may not resonate with my students. Fortunately, there are several things teachers can do to remedy this situation.

After I demonstrate or explain something, I like to turn things over to my students and put them in the leadership role. It's always interesting to see what happens when I ask students to demonstrate, as they may have a completely different idea of what I'm trying to achieve. Observing students' demonstration is a great way for me to find out what they think is going on. When we're both on the same path, it's great. When my demonstration misses the mark, I need to find another approach.

Similarly, it's interesting to see what happens when I ask for students' explanation. I'm interested to see what words they use to describe what's going on. I may discover that they have a completely different interpretation from mine. And I may find that students' choice of vocabulary reinforces their independence and ownership more naturally than my choice of words. In this way, I use demonstration and explanation to share ideas with students, in combination with students' own demonstration and explanation as confirmation of their independence and ownership.

When possible, I also ask for the same point at different moments during students' lessons. I might say something like, "What was the special idea in 'Twinkle Twinkle Little Star'? Can you show me one more time? What name did we call it? Thanks." Weaving such activities throughout the lesson means students may strengthen their potential for remembering what to do at home. This strategy increases students' potential to return the following week with ownership of details that occur during lessons.

Finally, I recognize there are many reasons why not everything will get done according to my plan. Sometimes, it's most important to be patient with students' growth.

Build On and Exercise What's Already There

Autonomy: our need to feel in charge.

1. In your teaching, what words or gestures might you take for granted that limit or deny students' autonomy?
2. How do you build on and exercise what's already there in terms of student autonomy?
3. What are the obstacles? What are your successes?
4. What is your takeaway from this exploration of autonomy?

NOTES

1. Susan Cain, *Quiet* (New York: Broadway Books, 2013).
2. Daniel Pink, *Drive: The Surprising Truth about What Motivates Us* (New York: Riverhead Books, 2009).
3. Lucy Green, *How Popular Musicians Learn* (Burlington, VT: Ashgate Publishing Company, 2002).
4. Dorothy Corkille Briggs, *Your Child's Self-esteem: The Key to Life* (Garden City, NY: Doubleday & Company, 1975).
5. See the following additional resources: Barbara Coloroso, *Kids Are Worth It* (Toronto, ON: Somerville House Publishing, 1995); Eric Jensen, *Super Teaching*, fourth edition (Thousand Oaks, CA: Corwin Press, 2009).
6. William Westney, *The Perfect Wrong Note* (Pompton Plains, NJ: Amadeus Press, 2003).
7. See the following additional resources: Janet Horvath, *Playing (Less) Hurt: An Injury Prevention Guide for Musicians* (Milwaukee, WI: Hal Leonard Books, 2010); Nancy Taylor, *Teaching Healthy Musicianship: The Music Educator's Guide to Injury Prevention and Wellness* (Oxford, UK: Oxford University Press, 2016); Judith Kleinman and Peter Buckoke, *The Alexander Technique for Musicians* (London: Bloomsbury, 2013); Aaron Ziegler and Michael M. Johns, "Health Promotion and Injury Education for Student Singers," *Journal of Singing* 68, no. 5 (2012) 531–41; Thomas Mark, *What Every Pianist Needs to Know about the Body* (Chicago: GIA Publications, 2003).

Chapter 7

Practicing and Fluency

Fluency is the need to feel personally effective/successful in acquiring competency and executing skills necessary to pursuits. It's the need for mastery of aspects in our own lives.

From MBT's Studio

Eight-year-old Ethan had arrived at an important destination in his music studies. Soon, in front of family and friends, he would perform his first solo concert of elementary piano pieces from memory. What could he do to get ready for this major undertaking? It seemed like he'd already done it all: playing with eyes closed, keeping a steady beat, breathing deeply into his core, keeping track of mistakes. What could he possibly do that he hadn't already done? Time was running out! Then it dawned on him. There was something he could do that he was certain no student had ever done before. Something that would set him apart from all the other students. For his final days of practice, Ethan tested himself in a way that indeed no other student ever had. Piece by piece, carefully at first and then with greater confidence, Ethan played each piece while standing on his right leg with his left leg crossed over. By all available standards, it was an incredible human accomplishment!

Andrew was the fourth of five siblings to take music lessons with me. He was also the fourth of five children to embrace his entire family's passion for ice hockey. After six years of lessons and Andrew entered junior high, I wasn't surprised when he informed me that his ice hockey training and games schedule would severely curtail his available time. Quitting music wasn't an option because it simply meant too much to him. What could I do to help him? "Please don't work hard," I advised Andrew. "If you think you need to work hard during your piano practice sessions, choose something small and limit yourself to five or ten minutes maximum." Over the next four years, as Andrew explored pieces from classical to popular to exams, my advice never wavered. "Please don't work hard" became our shared mantra, a reassurance that small amounts of intense piano practice could bring about the level of performance mastery to which Andrew had grown accustomed.

The stories of Ethan and Andrew demonstrate how students and teachers can work together to develop student fluency in musical performance while at the same time continuing the underlying theme of autonomy. In Ethan's case, we observe fluency resulting from his own autonomous need to self-direct. Knowing that he's not afraid to push his own limits, my role as teacher is to support and guide as appropriate. For Andrew, I support and guide while also being attentive to his time constraints.

This second aspect associated with practicing—fluency—is all about a person's basic need to feel successful in acquiring skills throughout their own life. Also described by words like "mastery" or "competency," fluency conjures up images of automaticity, of being able to do things spontaneously and without thinking. We typically acknowledge that fluency flourishes as a result of a person's desire to get better at something that matters to them.

According to Edward Deci and Richard Ryan, the need for competency leads people to seek challenges that are optimal for their capacities and to persistently attempt to maintain and enhance those skills and capacities through activity.[1] Competency exhibits itself through the individual's sense of confidence and effectiveness in action. Basic human needs for competency/fluency suggests that, whether or not people are explicitly conscious of such needs as goal objects, the healthy human psyche strives for them and, when possible, gravitates toward situations that provide them. When learning to sing or play a musical instrument, this idea provides a powerful explanation for the driving force behind practicing and our attempts to enhance our musical achievements.

Your Thoughts

Fluency refers to the ease a person has for performing a specific task or fulfilling a particular pursuit.

1. What are your own experiences with developing musical fluency?
2. Which experiences from your own personal autobiography contribute to how you develop your students' fluency?

THE ACTIVITY ITSELF

From an early age, children are well acquainted with the notion of fluency. They develop it intuitively and unassumingly by performing the activity itself. They develop fluency in speaking by speaking, walking by walking, dressing themselves by putting on their own clothes. However, when we take a closer look at such processes, we may see there's more going on than what's obvious at first glance. For example, competency in walking results not merely from the experience of walking, but from the person's success in walking safely from one location to another. Likewise, fluency in speaking isn't just a matter of making sounds. Fluent speech results from a person using the inflections, sounds, or words appropriate to successfully communicate. Developing fluency is a deeply embedded and multilayered undertaking that involves emotional, physical, and reflective processes in addition to personal meaning and social connections. Also important, as people repeatedly participate in activities, they may experience both increasing and regressing fluency. Fluency may come and go because it's not necessarily a fixed or inflexible state. It's characterized by a fluidity that ebbs and flows.

Music students naturally develop fluency similar to the way they achieve fluency elsewhere—by deliberately immersing themselves in the activity itself—mostly by playing through entire pieces or favorite sections thereof. For them, it's a no-brainer because previous accomplishments provide ample proof of their success with developing fluency by participating in the activity. At all stages of musical development, students play through their favored pieces or sections in order to experience and test out their level of musical fluency. They cannot resist because every time they play through a favorite piece it's like getting a pat on the back—a well-deserved emotional reinforcement. Therefore, they engage in playing pieces over and over again because it's emotionally fulfilling. It's so much fun to do!

Your Thoughts

Everyone enjoys repeatedly playing their favorite pieces.

1. How has the idea of repeatedly playing favorite pieces contributed to your own musical development?
2. Can you imagine your musical development without the impact of your favorite pieces?

As students develop increasing fluency, teachers may step in and assist students, by drawing their attention to the basics of music performance: tone, technique, and beat. (To be sure, non-keyboard musicians include an additional basic in terms of intonation.) Teachers help students to pay attention not only to the immediate aspects of skill development, but also to reflective processes that precede and follow their personal efforts. In other words, teachers encourage students to connect what they're doing with what they anticipate and observe in their performances. They help students plan for and recognize the basics of successful music performance much in the same way adults assist children when learning to walk and speak. That is, pointing out how successful walking is achieved when you're attentive to where you're stepping and how fluent speaking depends on the intricacies of pronunciation.

Teaching Tip

√ Use students' favorite pieces to generate fluency.

1. Utilize age- and level-appropriate strategies.
2. Explore basics of tone production, technique, and beat.
3. Have fun!

My focus on tone, technique, and beat is deliberate because they're fundamental elements in every piece of music. Reinforcing these basics at any level prepares students for mastery at the next higher level. This means that at every lesson, I facilitate age- and level-appropriate explorations[2] to help students develop greater awareness and fluency in terms of tone, technique, and beat. While I make sure students are having fun with their performances, I'm also responsible for helping them develop increasingly sophisticated ways of looking at what they do.

From MBT's Studio

In his second year of music lessons, Patrick's practice routine includes a reading workbook, a few new pieces, and several pieces previously mastered. From week to week, Patrick works with his teacher to come up with various ways to continue exploring his previously mastered pieces. Last week, when his pieces seemed to have lots of inconsistencies, they decided it would be good to play a "trial run" and "musical excellence" examples. This week, Patrick liked the idea of putting phrasing into each of the pieces. His teacher encouraged him to add his breath to make the phrasing more energetic. It seems there's potential for lots of exploration.

Over the years, I've come to realize that using students' preferences for playing their pieces or favorite sections to develop fluency has three distinct advantages. First, it means I start with what students like to do. I avoid the possibility that because students may dislike specific technical exercises, they'll develop a begrudging attitude to music or not practice at all. Second, this approach eliminates the gap between the development of fluency and its application. Students can tell whether they have sufficient fluency or not by its immediate application to the piece. Third, it allows me to reinforce students' closely held experience of fluency as something that develops by doing the activity itself. I validate students by confirming their own intuitive insight into lifelong learning. In other words, I develop fluency this way because students' attitudes matter to me, because shortcuts are desirable, and because of my respect for building on what students already know.

What stands out for me in this examination is that students' development of fluency doesn't take place in isolation. It occurs within an environment in which trial and error, celebration, disappointment, student peers, family involvement, listening to recordings, going to concerts, watching videos on YouTube, and more all have an impact on students' musical development. In such a dynamic environment, students' preference for playing their pieces or favorite sections is greatly influenced by everything that surrounds them. It's an activity they'll return to again and again, an activity they can't resist, and something they'll continue throughout their entire lives because playing pieces—no matter how successful or unsuccessful—confirms something essential and nonnegotiable about our involvement with music. That we can't get enough of the way music makes us feel. My role as teacher is to assist students by acknowledging their autonomy, leading when they need me, guiding when appropriate, and affirming students' awareness and appreciation of their own performances.

REPETITION

It seems safe to say that repetition plays an important role in developing fluency. We use repetition in order to achieve the automaticity that's associated with fluency, mastery, and competency. In my experience as a teacher, I've come to understand that it's possible to think about repetition from several different perspectives.

K. Anders Ericsson is a Swedish psychologist and researcher whose work in the area of human performance has received international recognition. In 1993, Ericsson, along with his colleagues Ralf Krampe and Clemens Tesch-Römer, came up with the term "deliberate practice" to describe the specific characteristics consistent with how experts practice. According to Ericsson's research,[3] expert performers across many domains maintain practice routines that are highly structured, optimize time and energy, rely on constant critical feedback, and use repetition of the same or similar tasks to overcome weaknesses with the explicit goal of improving performance. These experts make a commitment to structured practicing that is neither short-lived nor simple, typically involving an investment of ten thousand hours (2.8 hours daily) over a period of at least ten years. Deliberate practice involves a lot of focused repetition. Furthermore, Ericsson also notes how the effort required in deliberate practice means it is not an inherently enjoyable activity. Individuals are motivated to engage in deliberate practice because such practice improves their performance. Deliberate practice has important long-term considerations, mainly that the effort required for deliberate practice can only be sustained for a limited time each day without leading to exhaustion. To maximize gains from long-term practice, individuals must avoid exhaustion and limit practicing to an amount from which they can completely recover on a daily or weekly basis.

Your Thoughts

1. How do you feel about deliberate practice? For yourself? For your students?

2. What are some advantages? How about disadvantages?

What's most interesting about Ericsson's research is how it links back to the concept of autonomy; how deliberate practice depends on deep, self-generated personal involvement. Deliberate practice isn't just a matter of intense repetition. It's a developmental strategy that requires the individual's capacity for working on the task that's most personally challenging for themselves. If students want to improve what they're doing, they need to be the ones who generate the move. In my own teaching, deliberate practice has been important and practical for many of my senior students in preparing for upper level conservatory examinations. Without students' personal involvement, deliberate practice can easily turn into blind compliance with teacher's demands. As for my own musical journey, particularly during my years as a university student, I readily acknowledge engaging in a lot of deliberate practice in order to meet the heavy demands of multiple juries, solo concerts, and chamber recitals. It was the only way I could be certain to get everything done. However, when it comes to elementary and junior high school students, I have concerns that deliberate practice may have several unavoidable drawbacks.

First, deliberate practice can be an unenjoyable process, whereby people are motivated to practice because it improves their performance, not because they enjoy the process itself. I see this as a disadvantage with negative long-term implications because it encourages students to dislike what they're doing and disengage and detach themselves from the potential for satisfaction from musical development.

Second, deliberate practice focuses on improving student performance by eliminating their weaknesses rather than building on their strengths. Of course, there is merit in teachers helping students fix wrong notes or inaccurate rhythms. However, when it comes to the basics of musical performance, like tone production, technique, and beat, it seems advantageous and supportive for teachers to incorporate student's confidence with the successful basics in one piece as the building blocks for another.

Third, deliberate practice places its emphasis on achieving expertise through extraordinary amounts of repetitious practice. While this strategy may be vital for those students who pursue elite levels of competition, my students typically have no interest in such demanding explorations. For the most part, the expertise needed for elite competition doesn't represent what they're looking for or what they hope to achieve, not because they're incapable, but simply because they're more interested in enjoying the fruits of their labors than moving to a higher level of expertise. They commit to a level of music fluency or mastery that meets their own needs, which in most cases can be achieved with modest, rather than extreme, amounts of repetition. This means that for my elementary and junior high school students, I rarely use deliberate practice to assist with developing fluency. Instead, I prefer an approach to repetition that involves loosely structured activities aimed at stimulating students' enjoyment, creativity, and active participation. For intermediate and advanced students, like the example of my student Andrew, I suggest that brief and consistent amounts of hard work may suffice.

Teaching Tip

√ Use deliberate practice in manageable amounts.

1. Nurture students' fluency over time.
2. Build on and exercise what's working.
3. Be patient.

CREATIVITY AND CHALLENGES

From MBT's Studio

At a workshop master class, teenage Jessica steps forward, hands me her music, and asks, "Do I have to play it my teacher's way?" I reply, "No. I think we can start somewhere else. Why don't you show me what you've got?" After she's finished playing the piece, I say, "Thanks for that. Let's see what happens if we change things up a bit. I'm curious to see what it would sound like if you played a *blue* version of this piece." Jessica looks doubtful, so I add, "There's no right or wrong way. Let's see what your imagination has to offer." After she finishes playing the *blue* version, I say, "Thanks so much. How about a *red* version?"

I continue for several more interpretations, watching with great interest as Jessica excels at versions appropriate to pop stars Michael Jackson and Taylor Swift before I finally ask her to play it her teacher's way. My point is to help Jessica make refinements to her playing by starting with her own vitality, gradually progressing through her own imaginative resources, so that she might experience for herself how she has more than enough creativity and proficiency to accommodate multiple interpretations.

American pianist Paul Pollei (1936–2013) was a founding member of the American Piano Quartet and a devoted member of the piano faculty at Brigham Young University for four decades. During his lengthy performance and teaching career, Pollei performed internationally and actively contributed to the Music Teachers National Association, the National Conference on Piano Pedagogy, and the World Federation of International Music Competitions. Passionate about issues of piano pedagogy, Pollei was invited in 1991 by *The Piano Quarterly* to share his thoughts. Pollei used the opportunity to describe how his own youthful approach to practicing consisted of "improvising, fiddling, noodling, composing, sight reading anything and everything, and generally having a wonderful time at the piano"; and how his mother would shout from the kitchen, "You are not practicing your lesson!" Interestingly, Pollei's narrative describes what might be interpreted as the absence of deliberate practice, despite his mother's efforts to ensure adherence to the teacher's program of "exercises and disciplinary work."[4]

Writing from the vantage point of experience, Pollei placed a high value on his own self-imposed youthful rituals at the piano, even going so far as to "long for those kinds of students who initiate their own creative world of music-making."[5] Pollei had discovered something slightly unsettling about his university-level piano students in that many of them were so accustomed to following instructions that they struggled to move past their proven routines to explore something novel or new. Their success as performers and students was irrevocably attached to highly structured practice routines. Without such routines, they would most likely not have achieved their level of playing. However, by following such prescriptive structures, the spontaneity and creativity of their performances were severely jeopardized.

Reading Pollei's article, I couldn't help thinking that his self-directed, youthful ritual depicted the way I practiced in my own youth. My typical sessions at the piano consisted of adventures involving repeatedly moving from one piece to another, sight reading unexplored pieces, something old, maybe some scales or technique, something new, followed by my mom's interjection from the next room on behalf of my teacher. It seems that both Pollei and I were very much committed to our own self-determined rituals, even though our parents and teachers evidently endorsed disciplined approaches. We both developed fluency as musicians by repeatedly engaging in loosely structured, self-determined activities. We used repetition to develop fluency, but not necessarily in the way our teachers had in mind. Also, Pollei's consideration and concern for his students' creativity resonates with my own observations. I have noticed that while many of the students I taught in workshops displayed a superior performance level, many were so habituated in performing a piece "the right way" that they couldn't move past their own well-formed experiences to try something new. It's as if the deliberate repetition of all their efforts had formed a barrier against their own musical development.

Your Thoughts

Paul Pollei describes his youthful practicing as a mixture of "improvising, fiddling, noodling, composing, sight reading anything and everything, and generally having a wonderful time at the piano."[6]

1. How does Pollei's description compare with your own youthful practicing?
2. What about practicing did you most enjoy? Least enjoy?

Acknowledging that children today are much the same as when I was a child has had a huge impact on the way I teach. I willingly accept that my students most likely spend their time at the piano similar to my own loosely structured youthful adventures. Likewise, I'm keenly aware that my teaching may either lock or unlock students' musical development. So, how can teachers realistically help students develop fluency? How does repetition come into play?

My solution for the dilemma teachers face in teaching is to use a variety of challenges as tools for developing students' musical fluency. Challenges can come from students or myself. For challenges to be meaningful or enticing, they must display several characteristics. Challenges must be personally compelling, be appropriate for the student's age, and be suitable to the student's level of study. They guide the direction, intensity, and quality of an activity. They cannot be so easy that students will think they're useless or of no value. They cannot be so hard that students will have no chance of successful completion. Furthermore, it's important to incorporate a variety of challenges into practicing, given that what's challenging one minute may not be challenging the next. Mixing up challenges in practicing is highly beneficial. (For an extensive list of diverse challenges, see appendix A.)

As Benedict Carey points out in *How We Learn*, studies have shown that we learn more efficiently when presented with a "mixed bag of related tasks,"[7] no matter the age of the student or whatever the subject is. Carey asserts that our belief in repetition may be misplaced. It's not that repetitive practice is bad. We all need a certain amount of it to become familiar with any new skill or material. But repetition creates a powerful illusion. Skills improve quickly and then plateau. By contrast, varied practice produces a slower apparent rate of improvement in each single practice session but a greater accumulation of skill and learning over time. In the long term, repeated practice on one skill slows us down.

Teaching Tip

√ Change things up with a mantra of creativity and challenges.

   1. I'm curious to see what you can do.
   2. I'm curious to hear what you have to say.
   3. I'm curious to know what's on your mind.

The language associated with using challenges is remarkable in the way it invites students to actively participate in the repetitious process of developing fluency. From the onset of students' first lessons, I use specific language to introduce them to any number of challenges. I start with phrases like, "I'm curious to see if you . . . " knowing that it won't be long before I invite their active decision-making involvement with, "What challenges do you want to use?" This back-and-forth process of exploring and testing challenges helps students, and me, figure out what repetitions might, or might not, be valuable. Thus, repetition isn't something arbitrarily decided by teachers and imposed upon students. Repetition is what students use to develop fluency in performance as active participants in a shared teacher/student approach. Their mastery of piano performance emerges from teacher-guided adjustments to the intensity and scope of challenges, and more importantly, as a result of their own spontaneous explorations and freedom in deciding where to focus their efforts.

What stands out for me is how the dynamics of repetition completely change when teachers modify their approach from enforcing deliberate practice to promoting active student engagement. With deliberate practice, students are motivated to repetitious practice because it improves their performance. Whereas when students actively participate in challenging their own development, they have the potential to not only improve their performances, but also to derive immense enjoyment and satisfaction through such activities. In this way, incorporating repetition as fundamental to fluency is really about actively involving students. Repetition involves more than deciding how many times students should repeat an activity—whether it's a matter of five, ten, fifty, or one hundred repetitions. It's about teachers finding the ways to tap into students' desire to invest their own time, energy, and effort in something that matters to them.

REVIEW AND REFINEMENT

Of all the processes I incorporate in my teaching, review and refinement is the process I rely on the most to develop performance fluency. Based on way people develop spoken fluency through endless application of their accumulated vocabulary, review and refinement describes how teachers use students' accumulated repertoire—not just their most recent piece—to generate students' ongoing musical development. This process differs radically from traditional exam-based teaching where students may focus on four or five pieces for an entire year, with each year starting from a clean slate. Also in many traditional cases, students may confidently perform their repertoire only for a brief time compared to the extended period they spend learning new repertoire. In a review and refinement setting, students' accumulated repertoire serves as the ongoing foundation for learning new repertoire, similar to the way a person's accumulated vocabulary provides the secure backdrop for learning new vocabulary.

Here's what happens in a review and refinement process. For example, using a selection of ten pieces with elementary-level students, I start by helping them to learn, refine, and perform piece #1 over a period of time. Next, rather than dropping piece #1 in order to move on to piece #2, I assist them with ongoing review and refinement of piece #1 while they add piece #2 to their repertoire. Following students' successful performance of piece #2, I facilitate review and refinement of both pieces #1 and #2 while they add piece #3 to their repertoire, continuing in this manner until all ten pieces (or a reasonable number of them) are complete.

My responsibility in a review and refinement process is to exercise and build on students' accomplishments from previous weeks in every weekly lesson. Because I always exercise the material students have previously mastered, because every week I build on students' accumulated repertoire, students increasingly perform each aspect successfully. Over time—not overnight—a gradual strengthening or internalization of students' repertoire and skills takes place. And it's not long before the majority of students' successful review and refinement repertoire (or skills) outnumbers the minority of students' less-than-secure newest repertoire (or skills). Once students reach an appropriate number of pieces, and as students add new pieces to their practicing, it's always my responsibility to make sure the amount of accumulated repertoire is manageable. Too many pieces and students run out of time and incentives for practicing. Too few pieces and students' newest pieces don't benefit. There is a Goldilocks amount of accumulated repertoire that works for each student.

Teaching Tip

√ Use review and refinement to support students' fluency development.

1. Build on and exercise students' accumulated repertoire.
2. Stay away from the "same old, same old."
3. Provide appropriate follow-up.

The challenge with review and refinement is that playing the same accumulated repertoire, week after week, may result in loss of student interest. That's why successful repetitive learning activities have a clear dependence on teachers' ability to create engaging learning conditions that keep students actively involved. Eric Jensen, author of *Super Teaching*, proposes that teachers have within them "at any time, in any place, both the ability and the responsibility to create favorable learning conditions."[8] This means teachers use their insight and expertise to turn repetitious instructional activities into the magic of successful learning.

Students typically lose interest in review and refinement instruction as a result of two distinct occurrences. The first reason relates to their perception of learning activities as having "nothing new." Week after week, they experience their lessons as the "same old, same old." Teaching seems to be more about students enduring the discipline of repetition than about teachers finding novel ways to enliven repetitious processes. To counter this drawback, I fill my teaching with an endless stream of flexible explorations, using a wealth of energetic expressions that spring spontaneously from that day's lessons. For example, on the day Keenan shows up wearing his ice hockey jersey, we use the sport's energy to enliven our explorations. When Janine begins with a story of her diving competition that took place over the weekend, diving becomes the operative energetic theme. When I notice how bright the sun is shining, the brilliance of sunlight offers inspiration into exploring tone production, technique, concentration, and rhythmic continuity.

As Subramaniam affirms, teachers who find ways to make activities or tasks novel have a better chance of increasing students' interest and participation.[9] Using dynamic metaphors like the weather, holidays, colors, and more allows my students and me to come up with novel themes for each lesson. The whole point is to bring fresh energy to students' repetitious explorations while purposefully strengthening their habits of musical performance.

The second reason occurs when teachers fail to follow up on students' review and refinement pieces at their next lesson. Unfortunately, teachers who don't hear students' review and refinement pieces give students the impression these pieces aren't all that important. Students end up thinking it's their newest piece that deserves the most attention, while their efforts to improve the newest repertoire don't benefit from the habits gained in their accumulated review and refinement pieces. As a consequence, I often make a clear confirmation of how these pieces contribute to students' development, as demonstrated in the following scenario.

From MBT's Studio

After several months of music lessons, I wasn't certain eight-year-old Catherine understood how much her review and refinement pieces contributed to her ongoing progress. One week, I thought it would be interesting to make an inquiry.

"Catherine, your "Mary Had a Little Lamb" is amazing! It's got good tone, no mistakes, great legato. It's been one of your best pieces for months. You know it so well," I affirmed. "So, why do you think I ask you to play it at home every day? Why is it important to play 'Mary Had a Little Lamb,' one of your best pieces?"

The furrow in Catherine's forehead reflected her seriousness in considering my inquiry. A few moments passed as her father and I patiently waited. "So I won't forget," she replied with a simple yet summative assurance.

I appreciate how Catherine's emphasis on not forgetting succinctly captures the permanence essential to building successful habits of performance. When students' mastery of their accumulated repertoire is permanent, they have the capacity to take their newest pieces to higher levels.

Finally, I also appreciate how review and refinement means that students always have pieces ready for performance. They don't need to wait until the week before a concert to have a piece that's sufficiently polished to share with others. Furthermore, at the beginning of the school year in September, students typically have several pieces from the previous term that are still played moderately well. So we can get things up and running in a relatively short time period. They never need to go through the gruelling task of starting completely over again with a new group of pieces.

SLOW PRACTICE

In keeping with the idea of challenges discussed above, it occurs to me that an examination of slow practice may be relevant because it may easily be misinterpreted as a solution for any number of student issues related to fluency. Take a look at Jay's situation:

From MBT's Studio

Jay was a delightful elementary student who transferred to my studio after one year of study in another city. At her first lesson with me, she played several pieces, taking immense care in playing all her repertoire at a noticeably slow pace. The next week, while Jay persisted in her commitment to slow performances, I couldn't help notice how her pieces always contained several unexpected accidents—wrong notes, wrong fingerings, and wrong rhythms—that seemed to arrive completely out of the blue. As she moved from piece to piece, I counted to myself the number of accidents in each piece and discovered that Jay had on average a total of five to six accidents in each selection. "Thanks for the slow speed, Jay," I said. "Now I'm curious to see what happens with a quicker speed. Why not give that a try?"

What happened next was remarkable. Of course, it's tempting to think that Jay had no accidents at the quicker speed. However, when playing more quickly, Jay had only two or three accidents whereas at the slower speed she had five or six. When Jay played slowly, it was as if she lost track of where she was in the piece. She struggled to connect the slow tempo with her own internal sense of the piece. Over the next year, I encouraged Jay to continue playing at a comfortably quicker speed and the accidents gradually disappeared. As Jay's fluency developed, her ability to manage the demands of notes, fingerings, and rhythms also increased.

Jay's story is a good example of how slow practice may not offer students a reliable route to fluency because the natural speed of young children is quicker than adults. They breathe more rapidly. Their heart rate is faster. Therefore, it makes sense that young students will most likely want to play their pieces at a relatively quick tempo in keeping with their own internal impulse. For these reasons, slow practice deserves prudent consideration because its application can be problematic for young students.

Your Thoughts

1. What was your attitude to slow practice as a student?
2. How do you incorporate slow practice with your own students?

The danger with slow practice, according to piano pedagogue Jeffrey Swinkin, is that teachers may overlook "what the student is actually experiencing *while* playing slowly."[10] Although teachers may rely on slow practicing as a staple of their own experienced approach to learning, slow practice for students may introduce elements that are beyond students' capacity for control or understanding. They may actually be put at a disadvantage. As a rule, slow practice is highly beneficial in targeting small amounts of specific details in performance such as a beginner student's first efforts in playing one bar hands together or a junior student working on individual trills. However, for young students playing entire pieces, the benefits from slow practice may be overshadowed by the loss of students' own internal impulse and the reliance on an artificially imposed sense of beat, not to mention the stifling of creativity and musicality.

Teaching Tip

√ Speed up and slowdown in manageable degrees.

1. Use slow practice sparingly on entire pieces.
2. Utilize reasonable slower and quicker speeds to promote fluency.

While I encourage my students to use everything from excruciatingly slow to racing fast for targeting specific details in their performances, I consistently stay away from slow practice on entire pieces. Instead, I prefer cycles of manageable, slower and quicker performance speeds. My goal is to develop students' fluency by working in close proximity to the performance tempo. When and where necessary, I encourage students to use pauses to alleviate difficulties like the right hand chord changes in "Happy Farmer" or the finger position shifts in any scale passage, just like they might pause in speaking while searching for the right word. In this process, students avoid getting locked into any one tempo or style of performance. And, using a variety of explorations to develop student fluency may be more beneficial than a strict diet of slow practice.

IMMEDIATE AND EVOLVING

"Fluency," "mastery," and "competency" are self-affirming terms in the world of music that describe the successful acquisition and execution of skills related to learning to sing or play an instrument. What I've noticed in my own students is that fluency emerges in several different ways. On occasion, it seems like the student's fluency was already there, just waiting for us to tap into and put into play. This kind of fluency may be unexpected and is much appreciated, especially when students discover they can play a piece they didn't think they knew.

The kind of fluency that I spend the most time developing in my students tends to evolve over several days, weeks, and even months. It stands in stark contrast with the immediacy of twenty-first-century technology wherein we can get what we want just by clicking a button. Unfortunately, technology can give us a false impression of active involvement while inadvertently promoting subtle levels of impatience for activities that require more than the click of a button—like the fluency necessary for musical performance.

FAQs

Q: I have a colleague who uses a "100 Days Practice Club" to encourage consistent practicing with his students. When I tried it with my students, I found the results to be quite inconsistent. Some students participated enthusiastically. Others didn't. Is this a good idea or not?

A: There are lots of good things to be said about strategies like a "100 Days Practice Club." While allowing students to visibly keep track of their own achievement, this strategy rewards students for their commitment, persistence, consistency, dedication, discipline, and perseverance. All good things. However, as you point out, it's not necessarily a strategy that resonates with all students.

Strategies like this are worthwhile when they allow for diverse input. For example, some practices may include only doing things for fun; some may be less than five minutes; others may involve intense effort and discipline. In this way, students avoid falling into the habit of doing the same thing day after day. And they benefit from intentionally mixing up their practicing in keeping with learning strategies reported in books like *Make It Stick*[11] and *How We Learn*.[12]

My impression is that strategies like a "100 Days Practice Club" don't really tell the whole story. That is, students may maintain and even improve their playing without practicing every day. Don't get me wrong, I'm not saying students may maintain or improve their playing without any practice at all. What I am saying is that repetitious, daily practicing isn't the only way to develop fluency. Sometimes not practicing or taking a break and letting things settle is more beneficial than applying more effort. Of course, deliberately not practicing the week before a concert isn't advisable. I make sure my students know they have a better chance of performing well when they practice sensibly than when they don't practice at all.

Q: Repetition seems to be integral for developing fluency in learning to sing or play a musical instrument. How can teachers tell when students have enough fluency to move from one piece to the next?

A: I pay close attention to three important aspects: technical requirements, interpretive elements, and students' positive mindset.

Most often, students' mastery of technical requirements and interpretive elements is considered the measurement most appropriate for determining their readiness for moving on to the next piece. Students with skill sets equal or beyond the technical and interpretive demands of specific repertoire are considered fluently ready for the next level of difficulty. The benefit of using students' mastery as fluency measurement means that they may move easily from one level to another without undue hardship or duress. They make progress in a manageable step-by-step manner. The difficulty is that this approach doesn't take into consideration students' mindset during the process and that lengthy processes focused on technical and interpretive mastery may even be detrimental to a positive mindset. I want to avoid situations where working toward technical or interpretive mastery actually results in a deterioration of students' enthusiasm for learning. My thinking is that without students' positive involvement, they may take little satisfaction in their mastery. Without students' positive mindset, students' continuation may be in jeopardy.

I like to keep my students' positive mindset as a top priority at all stages of developing their musical fluency—along with technical and interpretive mastery. In this way, it's not fluency on its own that indicates when students move from one piece to the next. It's the combination of mindset, technique, and interpretation that informs how I guide students. This has important implications for review and refinement of students' accumulated repertoire in making sure I avoid staying too long on one piece (or group of pieces) so as not to let the student's positive mindset suffer. When students reach a plateau and progress seems to have ground to a halt along with their positive mindset, my response is to move on to fresh material. I'm not the least bit worried that students' musical fluency is tied exclusively to specific pieces in their accumulated repertoire. There are more than enough alternative options available to support students' musical development. My responsibility to students is to step in and help out before their positive mindset disappears completely and irrevocably.

Q: How do you use repetition as a tool to prepare students for concert performances?

A: Concerts are a great way for students to share their musical accomplishments with others. My approach to concerts is to remember that students may perform under various circumstances: spontaneous concerts, home concerts, studio concerts, and graduation concerts. Each concert setting has its own needs in terms of repetition and students' preparation.

Spontaneous concerts are performances that occur without any preparation. Right from the very first lesson, I encourage students to give frequent, spontaneous concerts to demonstrate what they've learned thus far, no matter how new. Spontaneous concerts are great settings for students to test out their new learning and determine their success with fresh repertoire. Students may also use spontaneous concerts for relaxed performances of repertoire with which they feel completely comfortable.

For formal home and studio concerts, I guide students with selecting and preparing for their performances. Two to three weeks prior to the concert, we select repertoire students already play at a high level of competency. Students may play an old piece or a new one, as long as their performance demonstrates sufficient performance refinement. The focus of concert preparation is that students engage in a breadth of challenges that stimulate and support high levels of musicianship (e.g., practicing the piece with and without the score, keeping the beat with one hand and playing with the other, practicing with eyes closed, practicing with diverse interpretations). (See the entire list of challenges in appendix A.)

I incorporate graduation concerts to mark the milestones of students' achievements. Whether teachers use ABRSM (Associated Board of the Royal Schools of Music) or RCM (Royal Conservatory of Music) exams, Suzuki repertoire, or other organized approaches, students perform a selection of repertoire appropriate to their development. Similar to home and studio concerts, I guide students with their preparation. Graduation concerts involve repetitious cycles over extended periods of time.

In students' final year with me, I encourage them to put together a final concert performance tailored to their own interests. Here are some examples:

- Ethan sang and accompanied himself on a collection of popular songs by Billy Joel, Sean Mendez, Ruth B., and Leonard Cohen.

- Anna performed *Clair de Lune* by Debussy, *Sonata K545* by Mozart, and selections from Billie Eilish.

- Jenna performed *Waltz* by Chopin, themes from the *Mary Poppins* musical, and *Sound of Music*.
- Brandon performed all the repertoire and etudes for his RCM Grade Nine piano exam.

Q: I have noticed something in a few students and I'm not sure how to respond. The situation is the student plays a piece during their lesson that seems to have noticeable improvements since the previous week. I respond by saying, "Nice job. That piece has really improved. Thanks for practicing so hard." The student replies, "Oh. I didn't practice this piece at all last week." Can you tell me what's going on?

A: It can be mind-boggling to understand how, on occasion, students may play well with no practice. What seems challenging is the assumption that successful performances are the result of dedicated practice. Of course, there's a certain logic to this statement, so teachers encourage students to work hard and diligently practice because we recognize how it contributes to successful performances. However, we might be more accurate if we said something like, "Successful performance may be the result of focused practice, practicing outside the box, and taking a break."

My approach to the above-described situation is to be proactive with students. This means that before they perform, I prefer to say something like, "Tell me what's going on in your Chopin this week." That way, I get pertinent information before the student performs rather than after. On occasion when I forget to be proactive, I inquire into their process by saying something like, "Nice job. Tell me what you did last week." That way, if they didn't practice at all, we can talk about what to do next because most likely, we agree that another week with no practice will not result in noticeable improvements.

Build On and Exercise What's Already There

Fluency: our desire for mastery.

1. In your own teaching, how does building on and exercising what's already there have an impact on students' fluency?
2. How much does your teaching rely on deliberate practice?
3. What can you do to incorporate a broad range of challenges into your students' practicing?
4. How does the strategy of review and refinement show up in your teaching?

NOTES

1. Edward Deci and Richard Ryan, *Handbook of Self-determination Research* (Rochester, NY: University of Rochester Press, 2002).

2. Vocal and instrumental instructors will want to pay close attention to the various voice-specific and instrument-specific aspects of performance.

3. K. Anders Ericsson, R. Krampe, and C. Tesch-Römer, "The Role of Deliberate Practice in the Acquisition of Expert Performance," *Psychological Review* 100 no. 3 (1993): 363–406.

4. Paul Pollei, "Our Evolving Profession," *The Piano Quarterly* 39 no. 153 (1991): 54–55.

5. Ibid.

6. Ibid.

7. Benedict Carey, *How We Learn: The Surprising Truth about When, Where, and Why It Happens* (New York: Random House, 2015).

8. Eric Jensen, *Super Teaching*, third edition (San Diego, CA: The Brain Store, 1995): 114.

9. P. Subramaniam, "Unlocking the Power of Situational Interest in Physical Education," *Journal of Physical Education, Recreation, & Dance*, 81 no. 7 (2010): 40.

10. Jeffrey Swinkin, *Teaching Performance: A Philosophy of Piano Pedagogy* (Dordrecht, Netherlands: Springer Publications, 2015).

11. P. C. Brown, H. L. Roediger, and M. A. McDaniel, *Make It Stick: The Science of Successful Learning* (Cambridge, MA: Harvard University Press, 2014).

12. Benedict Carey, *How We Learn*.

Chapter 8

Practicing and Purpose

Purpose is the need to feel that our personal efforts or pursuits are meaningful and the need to create things that are vital for our own lives. It also includes the need for positive interactions around musical experiences.

This third aspect associated with practicing is all about a person's basic need to do something that matters. Knowing about our purpose in practicing is important because it's easier to do something exceptionally well when we understand why we're doing it. For Daniel Pink, purpose provides balance for the aspects of autonomy and mastery/fluency. Pink affirms the most deeply motivated people—not to mention those who are most productive and satisfied—connect their desires to a cause larger than themselves.[1] Purpose is what activates our energy for living. It provides the goals and words for directions we might take.

Founder of the positive psychology movement, Martin Seligman makes strong connections between personal well-being and "belonging to and serving something that you believe is bigger than the self."[2] Often, we pursue purpose for its own sake because it provides meaning to our lives that goes beyond logic or reasoning. Stephen Covey frames the notion of purpose as beginning with the end in mind. Starting with a clear understanding of your destination means "to know where you're going so that you better understand where you are now and so that the steps you take are always in the right direction."[3]

In the context of learning to sing or play a musical instrument, purpose involves a mental or imagining creation that serves as the preparation for a physical or active creative rendering. We work with ideas as the inspiration for bringing depth and meaning to our musical performances. When purpose becomes a routine element in practicing, students find out what it feels like to align their thought processes, emotions, and values with their actions and intentions in the real world.

With purpose on my mind, many years ago I asked my students to write down their thoughts regarding musicianship and artistry. My fifteen-year-old student Drew wrote the following reflective essay:

From MBT's Studio

To me, musicianship and artistry are very similar, but also very different. I believe musicianship is having the ability to play music as it is written and being able to make it sound beyond what the writer could have ever imagined. Artistry, on the other hand, is being able to play the music but in your very own unique way to make it sound maybe better or just different than what the writer intended. Out of these two definitions that I gave, artistry is definitely my favorite. Don't get me wrong, I love to play music the way it's made and make it sound amazing. But, I think the word artistry pushes people past their limits. There is just something if someone tells you to put artistry in a piece that just makes it special. To me, it's like a window of opportunity, because you're playing a piece and it sounds astonishing. Then someone asks you to put artistry in, and in my head, I'm saying here's my chance to push myself above and beyond my limits. Sometimes it sounds great. Sometimes it doesn't, but in the end it doesn't really matter because you're just trying something new. Now musicianship, one of the greatest things is being able to master a piece which I believe is a great part of musicianship. I like to think I master all my pieces, but in reality I probably learn 1–2 songs a year that I get to the point of "mastering" which is a very proud feeling. I love both the words musicianship and artistry, and they have both helped me a lot through my years of music.

In the years since Drew crafted this essay, I've often wondered what specifically happened during his lessons that might have prompted such a thoughtful account. What did we talk about? How did he come to his insightful interpretations of musicianship and artistry? Somehow in the weeks and years of lessons, Drew pulled out his own sense of purpose from our many conversations. In this chapter, I explore what some of those conversations around purpose may have touched on.

Your Thoughts

Learning to sing or play a musical instrument may resonate with multiple purposes.

1. What purpose do you think your own teachers followed when you were a student?
2. What purposes would you like to pass on to your students?

MUSICIANSHIP AND ARTISTRY

When I was a child, I formed a trio with my two brothers. I played the piano along with my older brother, who played saxophone, and my younger brother who played trumpet. Tijuana brass music was popular in those days, so we routinely performed "A Taste of Honey," "Tijuana Taxi," and anything else that we could put together. Looking back on those years, it seems like we played a lot of concerts and that we enjoyed the reputation we gained from performing. People referred to us as the young "musicians" and we eagerly accepted the designation. We were musicians—not just kids who played musical instruments.

Terms like "musician" and "artist" carry many unspoken meanings, conjuring up images of creativity, exploration, and originality. Musicians and artists may be reputed for breaking the rules or working well outside the box of conventionality. Yet they also embrace the aspect of stewardship in carrying forward and passing on musical and artistic traditions. In comparison, the term "student" denotes all kinds of informal and formal engagements with learning. "Student" is a word synonymous with terms like trainee, or recruit, or apprentice that typically rely on teachers for direction and guidance. So when it comes to a musical setting, who do music teachers work with—students or musicians? It's an interesting question to consider because teachers' interactions with their students may draw significantly from whether teachers consider their job in terms of teaching students or teaching musicians. When teachers acknowledge that they give lessons to musicians, they underscore that their students—as music makers, artists, performers, and explorers—have something authentic and personal to say.

The words "musician" and "artist" constantly circulate through my studio with a noticeable impact on teacher/student interactions. Take a look at the following scenarios:

Scenario 1: After a junior level student's performance, the teacher says, "What a confident performance! Now, it would be fun to see what happens when you exaggerate your dynamics."

Scenario 2: After a junior level student's performance, the teacher says, "What a confident performance! Now, it would be fun to see what happens when you put in your own artistry."

Without a doubt, both statements have an impact on the student's subsequent efforts. Of course, the value of each statement may have specific intentions depending on the context of instruction. In one case, students' awareness of their dynamics may be in relation to an upcoming examination. In another case, it may be valuable for teachers to stimulate student's readiness for creativity. Each choice of words conveys a subtly different message. The first statement gives advice that seems relatively straightforward for a junior level student to implement. The teacher has indicated something concrete for the student to keep in mind. Whereas the second statement invites the student to explore without saying exactly what that exploration might look like. The teacher gives directions that are abstract and open to the student's discretion.

Most assuredly in each of the above examples, teachers know that junior-level students have the ability to play with exaggerated dynamics. What separates them is that the second teacher demonstrates interest in finding out more about what the student's musicianship and artistry sound like. Rather than limiting teacher/student interaction to something the teacher already knows as in Scenario 1, the second teacher uses the opportunity to gain further insight into what the student may bring into their performance.

Your Thoughts

Musicianship and Artistry

1. How do you feel about using these words to describe your students?
2. What messages do these words convey to students?

Music teachers may hesitate to make open-ended requests for musicianship or artistry because they worry that students will merely choose to play fast and loud. While I concur that fast and loud performances may not be the most enjoyable interpretations for teachers to listen to, my response is to say something like, "Well, I can certainly understand why you enjoy playing like that! It's totally full of energy." Then, I continue with another request, "Let's see what happens when you use your artistry to play this piece a different way. Or try my favorite way or the composer's," followed by an encouraging smile. I'm always astonished by the results because students have consistently demonstrated an uncanny and intuitive understanding of my own (and the composer's) favorite interpretation. Even students in workshops, who've only known me for five minutes, have successfully used their own artistry to explore what they think I might like.

Teaching Tip

√ Empower students to express their musicianship and artistry.

1. Start with open-ended requests.
2. Explore student's, teacher's, and composer's favorite.

Explorations involving musicianship and artistry are important in my teaching because I want to hear what students have to say. I encourage students to tap into their own musicianship and artistry because without self-expression their musical performances are incomplete. Knowing that musicianship and artistry can easily be overshadowed by the technical demands of performance and perfectionistic expectations, I make certain there's always time and space for students to express themselves. As a result of such explorations, I've come to understand that musicianship and artistry aren't like precious antique objects whose rarity or fragility means that only experts should handle them. Nor are they narrowly defined concepts that demand strict adherence to some sort of ordered musical system. Musicianship and artistry are open-ended and abstract impulses that thrive in students who put them into use but may remain dormant in students who don't. My responsibility as a teacher is to create a safe and supportive environment for nurturing the students' musicianship and artistry that's already there. In my studio, musicianship and artistry aren't token, well-intentioned expressions. They're fundamental elements that help me direct and guide students so they may experience for themselves the purpose of learning to play the piano: that is, their own multi-faceted, unconditional, and authentic experience of self-expression.

BEAUTY

Throughout history, beauty is one of the most enduring and controversial themes to occupy the minds of musicians. It is traditionally linked to aesthetics, taste, art, and cultural values. Philosophers associate beauty with the ultimate ideals of goodness, truth, and justice. In many traditional contexts, there's somewhat of an elevated reverence for beauty that imperceptibly distances it from our daily lives. However, we can all identify beauty in the everyday experiences of life. We see beauty captured in a baby's smile, the color of autumn leaves, and the sparkle in fresh snow. We hear beauty in the greeting of a loved one, the pealing of bells, the songbird's call, and the silent calm of a winter evening. So, what exactly happens when we experience beauty? How can we more fully understand the sense of appreciation, satisfaction, or pleasure that we associate with experiencing it?

In his book *The Divine Proportion*, H. E. Huntley highlights what he refers to as "three flavors" that prompt a person's awareness or appreciation of beauty: surprise, curiosity, and wonder.[4] As surprise, beauty is unanticipated, unexpected, and interruptive. An encounter with it has an arresting quality that grabs a person's attention, however subtle or direct, and a quality of delight that relates to discovery and creation. As curiosity, beauty invites exploration.

The person craves to know more, to get closer. As wonder, beauty opens unexplored words. It invites contemplation and instills transcendence. Beauty evokes an element of freedom, of being spiritually transported. Huntley's combination of surprise, curiosity, and wonder has a refreshing simplicity that's practical yet insightful.

From MBT's Studio

A performance by my adult student Karin brings Huntley's insight to mind. Although most of her repertoire typically includes meticulous dynamic indications, on this occasion, I asked Karin to choose either surprise, curiosity, or wonder as the guiding thought for her performance. As I listened to her interpretation, I was intrigued by the vitality of the performance. It was full of energy, unpredictable, rough around the edges at times, yet also pleasantly satisfying. All in all, Karin had achieved something quite beautiful and I felt privileged to share in her accomplishment.

What I appreciate about Huntley's combination of surprise, curiosity, and wonder is that beauty is something that we experience for ourselves. We're able to recognize beautiful musical performances when we hear them because we know what surprise, curiosity, and wonder feel like. Each of these experiences comes with an energy and intensity that are reflective of our active personal involvement. So, while beautiful music may be captured on video, in musical scores, on CDs or DVDs, on the internet, and in concert performances, I agree with the American philosopher Crispin Sartwell's statement that "we give beauty to objects and they give beauty to us; beauty is something that we make in cooperation with the world."[5] In this way, beauty flourishes in our responses to it and thrives in our actively creating it.

Teaching Tip

√ Exercise surprise, curiosity, and wonder.

1. Let go of prescribed interpretations.
2. Allow freedom for students to explore.
3. Connect beauty with real-life experiences.

CARING FOR MUSIC

From MBT's Studio

Nine-year-old Emily had been my student for five years. During that time, I'd learned that if I was going to ask her a question, I needed to make sure it was one worth answering. So, in responding to a particularly poor performance, I took my time to find the right words. "Emily, why do you think sometimes kids play well and sometimes they don't?" I asked. She shrugged her shoulders. "Well . . . kids who play well, want to," she began. "And kids who don't, don't really care," followed by another shrug of her shoulders.

With all my years of teaching, it's hard to believe I never considered that "not really caring" about how something turned out could have such an obvious outcome. It makes sense that if people don't care about whether they play well or not that it will show up in their performances. Why had I not figured this out on my own? How many poor performances had I misdiagnosed that were actually the result of "not really caring?" How was I going to get Emily to care about what she was doing? As it turned out, the solution was as direct as my initial question. I asked, "Could you play it with care?"

Ever since Emily told me about her thoughts on caring, I've shared her honest insight with other students on numerous occasions. I talk about caring for music because I want students to understand that musical performances rely on our care. Unlike the finished products of recordings or musical scores, our musical performances emerge spontaneously and almost fleetingly from each of us while anchored in the nuanced moments of our own complex lives—from the playfulness of a musical joke to the seriousness of a national anthem, from the affirmations of faith in church hymns to what's trending in pop music.

Teaching Tip

√ Care for music.

1. Shape performances with emotional expression.
2. Draw from the energy of our breath.
3. Make music in service of a larger cause.

Caring for music comes with the acknowledgment that both music and caring are things that give purpose to our lives. Without a doubt, we value music because of what it brings to our lives. Most of us can't even begin to imagine what life would be like without music. Similarly, we also value the aspect of caring because life without being cared for or caring for others seems to paint a grim picture. Our capacity for caring begins with the simple awareness that something or someone needs our caring involvement. Caring springs from our willingness to respond unconditionally as a matter of our own free will. Caring may even stretch our own boundaries and require levels of creativity and involvement previously unimagined.

Your Thoughts

In what ways does the exploration of caring for music impact your teaching?

Music has much to offer, from beauty and enjoyment to entertainment and distraction. When we care for music, it means doing something well, doing something as a privilege. It means we give what we can to openly communicate the enormity that music brings to our lives. Something larger than ourselves.

VISION OF LIFE

From 1983 to 1986 I studied with Dr. Shinichi Suzuki, founder of the Suzuki method, as a teacher apprentice at the Talent Education Institute in Matsumoto, Japan. Upon my graduation in May 1986, Dr. Suzuki presented me with a certificate written in Japanese calligraphy on which he had inscribed,

美しき 音に いのち を
Beautiful tone with living soul, please.

Translated from the Japanese *"Utsukushiki oto ni inochi o,"* "Beautiful tone with living soul, please" is a phrase Suzuki often intoned during my three-year apprenticeship. His signature statement is noteworthy because, although it's fairly straightforward to translate the Japanese words *utsukushiki* and *oto* into "beauty" and "tone," respectively, Suzuki takes special care in his translation of the Japanese term *inochi* as "living soul."

Dating from the eighth century, the term *inochi* has become established as one of the most popular words in the Japanese language.[6] Made up of *i* and *chi*, the former standing for "breath" and the latter for "dynamic energy," *inochi* is the word Japanese people use to express "life" as experienced through the interconnected wholeness of living and the mystery of irreplaceable energy shared by all living creatures. When Japanese talk about *inochi*, they're not just referring to the biological phenomenon westerners typically associate with the word "life." They're referring to a vision of life that embraces connections between the physical and the spiritual, life and death, from the individual to the universal, and beyond space and time. In his translation of *inochi* as "living soul," Suzuki attempts to capture the breadth of meanings associated with this word. He advocates a vision of life in which the interconnected mysteries of life resonate with spiritual awareness of the world around us.

While the English language has no equivalent to the Japanese concept of *inochi*, my efforts to include the term as an instructional element has meant developing appropriate and flexible language to talk about visions of life in ways my students can understand. Knowing that my own spiritual background may have little in common with my students, I tell stories about the spiritual connections many people feel toward music. I talk about the interplay of spirituality and self-expression found in generations of composers, performers, and music instructors whose spiritual devotion serves as meaningful anchors. I facilitate discussions that build on who I perceive my students to be and their capacity for connecting emotionally, spiritually, physically, and intellectually with the world around them. So, it's not unusual for me to ask students to put their "heart and soul" into their performances, to consider what it might be like to invite the "spirit of the universe" into their music making. Nor is it unusual to ask them what they think about the world around them, how they consider notions of spirituality and our interrelated universal connections.

Teaching Tip

√ Encourage students in exploring mysteries of the universe.

1. Find out how students connect with the world around them.
2. Make connections between self-expression and spirituality.
3. Play with heart and soul.

My impression is that learning to sing or play a musical instrument draws naturally and intuitively from the thoughts, beliefs, values, and attitudes we carry forward. Musical performance and study provide each of us with the opportunity to contemplate and explore the big picture, to develop awareness of the deeply rooted and soul-stirring ideals of life that empower who we are. (Relevant materials and suggestions devoted to such explorations are coming up in part 4, Character.)

REAL-LIFE STORIES

This chapter has explored four dynamics related to the purpose of practicing that may fuel our pursuit of meaningful directions. Quite interestingly, these four dynamics—musicianship and artistry, beauty, caring for music, and visions of life—share a remarkable characteristic of double-sidedness. On one side, they're definable and identifiable. They're things that we can experience objectively and with certainty. Without too much effort, we can generate accurate descriptions of musicianship and artistry, beauty, caring, and life vision. Yet, on the other side, they're are also strikingly abstract and open-ended. They entail a certain amount of creativity and imagination. No matter how much time or effort we put into exploring these four dynamics, we may never fully know or understand everything they have to offer. This double-sidedness has amazing implications because it means that the purpose of practicing isn't limited to exploring what's objectively definable or identifiable. It's also about broadening our ventures into what we have yet to imagine, into what we have yet to learn. So, what can teachers do to create the conditions for the as-yet unimagined? How might teachers open up more spaces for exploring the abstract and undefined?

My approach to the as-yet unimagined is to use stories to bridge the abstract and undefined with the recognizable events of daily life. I use real-life stories so that students may anchor their understanding of the unknown in actual real-life experiences. Over the years, I've become a kind of story gatherer. I tell stories from my own teaching and personal life in order to jostle, inform, soothe, wake up, stretch, test, entertain, and nurture my students. I also tell stories from my students that demonstrate who they are while embodying the respect and admiration I have for them. That's why most of my students are familiar with the story of my student Emily's insight into caring. Other stories originate in ideas and lives from the musical community of composers, historical figures, and contemporary icons. My responsibility is to keep stories safe, to value and protect them, and pass them on. It's as if I've become a steward of stories.

Your Thoughts

What stories do you tell that might help students bridge the unimagined with the experiences of real life?

What seems significant is that I use stories as my way of inviting my students to develop their own interpretations of the abstract. I provide my students with real-life portrayals of musicianship and artistry, beauty, caring for music, and visions of life so that they may hold onto and reinterpret their own understanding long after the stories have been told.

FAQs

Q: At the beginning of this chapter, you included a written response from your student Drew. How often do you use this strategy?

A: Once a year I gather written responses from students eleven years of age and older. I'm hoping to get a sense of my students' personal development in addition to our typical spoken interactions. By this age, students generally have adequate writing skills to complete this task. For their first reflection, I like to ask students, "What's it like for someone your age to learn to play the piano?" For older students, I use a different question every year. Some of the questions I've used in the past include, "What does musicianship and artistry mean to you? What is your takeaway from piano lessons after all these years? What advice would you give to another student taking music lessons?"

Q: I'm not sure I'm ready to talk about musicianship and artistry, beauty, caring, and life vision with my students. How did you first incorporate them in your teaching?

A: While all the above topics come from my own personal experience, implementation did not always follow a smooth or direct route. For example, during my studies in Japan, it was not unusual to hear Dr. Suzuki use the phrase, "Beautiful tone with living soul." However, when I returned to teach in Canada, I felt unsure about using such language. I was aware that Canadian school teachers were being encouraged to remove what might be perceived as spiritual bias from their language. So I responded accordingly. That all changed when I was invited to teach a series of piano workshops in a faith-based community. Working closely with teachers, students, and parents, I observed the obvious importance of their faith and how it permeated their lives. Suddenly, I could see the inauthenticity of neutralizing my teaching language. It was just the impetus I needed to include transcendent beliefs, personal values, and visions of life in my teaching language.

I started using the language of musicianship and artistry in my teaching after being inspired by a colleague's approach. Although my colleague made it look easy and natural, what struck me immediately was that it didn't feel easy or natural. Even though I had a clear understanding of musicianship and artistry in my mind, it was a completely different matter to get the words to come out of my mouth. I needed to practice using the language of musicianship and artistry. The only way I could get comfortable with the words was to start using them.

My fascination with beauty seems to be something that's always been part of my personal outlook. Books like Huntley's *The Divine Proportion*[7] have been immensely helpful. And the idea of caring for music—I have my nine-year-old student Emily to thank for her astute observation.

Moments of musicianship and artistry, beauty, caring, and vision of life may show up randomly and intentionally in every music lesson. For me, noticing those moments is where the language launching point occurs. Keeping eyes and ears open. Picking up and identifying the nuances in students' performances. Things like the flow of the piece, or dynamics, or concentration, or phrasing, even if these elements only appear for a matter of seconds. It's not necessarily about looking for consistency throughout the entire piece. When students are going in a good direction—no matter how briefly—it's important to let them know.

Build On and Exercise What's Already There

Purpose: the need to bring positive value to learning activities. This exploration included the topics: musicianship and artistry, beauty, caring, vision of life, and real-life stories.

1. The above topics resonate with the author's own background. What topics from your own background feel appropriate for this kind of exploration? What topics do you already build on?
2. How can you exercise topics that represent the diversity in your teaching studio?
3. What topics would you like to add on?

NOTES

1. Daniel Pink, *Drive: The Surprising Truth about What Motivates Us* (New York: Riverhead Books, 2009).
2. Martin E. P. Seligman, *Flourish: A Visionary New Understanding of Happiness and Well-being* (New York: Atria Paperback, 2011).
3. Stephen Covey, *The Seven Habits of Highly Effective People: Restoring the Character Ethic* (New York: Free Press, 2003).
4. H. E. Huntley, *The Divine Proportion* (New York: Dover Publications, 1970).
5. Crispin Sartwell, *Six Names of Beauty* (London, UK: Routledge, 2004).
6. M. Morioka, "The Concept of 'Inochi': A Philosophical Perspective on the Study of Life," *Japan Review 2* (1991): 83–115.
7. Huntley, *The Divine Proportion*, 1970.

Chapter 9

Practicing and Relatedness

Relatedness is the need to feel that our personal efforts or pursuits are socially connected/integrated and relevant to the surrounding social context; the need to participate in our world; the need for positive relationships; the desire to belong and be accepted as a member of a significant social grouping.

From MBT's Studio

After a home concert involving a small number of my students, the families gathered in the kitchen for refreshments. The children quickly grabbed their favorite treats and headed outdoors to enjoy the beautiful weather. Left on their own, the parents' discussion turned to the perennial topic of raising children. The lively discussion progressed through the challenges and rewards associated with school, piano practice, sports, and daily life. Karl, one of the fathers, asked another father, Leon, "What are you hoping your child will get from piano lessons with Dr. Thompson?" Indeed, I did wonder what were parents hoping to get from having their child study with me. It was an intriguing question with infinite ways of responding personally and professionally. Without a moment's hesitation, Leon responded, "I'm hoping that Dr. Thompson will phone the boys when they're in university." The simplicity and significance of Leon's statement has been long lasting. I continue to call his two boys from time to time to catch up on their latest developments.

Kyle entered my studio with the long-limbed movements of a growing thirteen-year-old boy. He handed me his books and asked, "Dr. Thompson, do you think you'll ever get mad at me?" All I could think was, How many people had gotten mad at Kyle that day? Possibly his teachers at school? His friends? His parents? Maybe even his sister had gotten mad at him? What about Kyle himself? Had he gotten mad at someone that day? Finally, I replied, "Kyle, for me, getting mad at someone probably isn't ever my first choice. But I wouldn't be honest if I said that I've never gotten mad at anyone, because I have. What might be important to know is that people typically get mad at someone when they think they've run out of options. When they can't think of anything else to do. So, on the day when I think I've run out of options for helping you, that most likely will be the day I get mad at you."

The stories of Leon and Kyle illustrate how music studies are characterized by the social and personal aspects of relatedness. In Leon's story, the relationship between teacher and students is something highly valued by the parent. This cherished relationship has longevity. It continues well beyond the years of music lessons while most definitely depending on the integrity established during the many years of teacher/student interaction. In Kyle's story, there's a vulnerability that calls for honesty and trust in the interaction between teacher and student. My responsibility as teacher is to acknowledge my role in fostering supportive educational relationships and supporting the relatedness that underpins students' musical and personal development.

One of the most basic needs we have as human beings is for relationships with others. It's as if we're predestined with a universal disposition for positive social interaction whether it comes from family, school, in the workplace, with neighbors, or from communities joined by sports, culture, or religion. Deci and Ryan describe relatedness as feeling connected to others, to caring for and being cared for by those others, to having a sense of belongingness both with other individuals and with one's community.[1] Relatedness reflects the tendency to connect with and be integral to and accepted by others. In this way, relatedness refers to a person's basic need to feel socially connected and integrated, to feel that their efforts are relevant and valued by members of the person's surrounding networks.

TEACHERS AND STUDENTS

From MBT's Studio

Chloe began her studies at age five and continued with me until she graduated from high school. Of the many students I've taught in my entire career, Chloe stands out as the most shy individual I've ever met—so shy that during the first two years of her lessons, she never spoke a single word to me. Throughout that time, according to her mother, Chloe spoke to no one outside her immediate family, not even her teachers or classmates at school. To ensure her active participation during those first years of complete silence on Chloe's part, I asked all kinds of questions that she could answer by nodding or shaking her head yes or no.

As time went by and years passed, Chloe's communication gradually evolved. The move from "yes" or "no," to single descriptive words, to sentences, spanned an entire decade. During the slow passage of years, I continued to honor our relationship by teaching in ways that she could respond, knowing that in a genuinely safe and supportive environment, Chloe would most assuredly flourish. The last time I checked in with Chloe, she was in her final year of earning a bachelor's degree, living on her own in another city, and running her own entrepreneurial business venture that employed other students as tutors. Her success brings a smile to my face.

Relatedness highlights that while students most obviously benefit from teachers' knowledge and expertise, students' practicing is also influenced by their relationships with teachers. A negative environment may impede students' practicing, whereas, a positive climate may energize their desire and success in practicing. This means that practicing isn't just an intellectual or emotional undertaking. Nor is it a neutral activity that takes place in a vacuum. Practicing is shaped by the quality of relatedness.

Your Thoughts

Relatedness is enhanced when teachers demonstrate awareness, acceptance, concern, criticality, safety, and stimulation. Research suggests these aspects increase students' creativity, reflection, and satisfaction.

How did the notion of relatedness show up in your experience as a student? What was the outcome?

In his book *Freedom to Learn*,[2] American psychologist Carl Rogers (1902–1987) examines the interpersonal relationship between teacher and student. Rogers's work in the field of psychotherapy is especially noteworthy for his humanistic approach and the way he valued the person's worth, dignity, and capacity for self-direction if given the proper environment. Through his years of careful research, Rogers verified the notion that a safe, supportive environment allowed each person to journey down the path of self-discovery, self-esteem, and self-directed learning. Although most of Rogers's early work centered on psychotherapy, he soon realized that his research had immense application to education, what he termed a "person-centered" approach to education as experienced in the relationship between teacher and student.

On the one hand, according to Rogers, successful teachers possess an insightful awareness and unconditional acceptance of their students. They are facilitators of learning with the extraordinary capacity for "prizing" the student. Whether we call it prizing, acceptance, trust, or some other term, Rogers championed prizing as a way of highlighting the teacher's attitude toward the student's feelings, opinions, and personhood. Prizing entails caring for the student, but in a non-possessive way. It requires acceptance and trust of the student as a separate person with their own rights. Teachers who "prize" their students can accept their occasional apathy, erratic desires to explore byroads of knowledge, as well as the student's disciplined efforts. They acknowledge that students come with personal feelings that may both disturb and promote learning. Students come with many feelings and much potential.

Teaching Tip

√ Embrace students in their entirety: feelings, opinions, and personhood.

1. Teachers accept and care for students as real persons.
2. Teachers accept and care for themselves as real persons.

On the other hand, Rogers also felt that successful teachers are vitally aware and accepting of themselves as persons. They present an attitude of "realness" or "genuineness" to students without a front or facade. They are themselves, not in denial of themselves. Teachers who are genuine can be enthusiastic, bored, interested, angry, sensitive, and sympathetic because they accept these feelings as their own, without the need to impose them on their students. When teachers who are genuine come into direct personal encounters with students, when they meet their students on a person-to-person basis, their facilitation of learning is more likely to be effective. From Rogers's point of view, we see that relatedness is about teachers setting up an environment where there's a "prizing" both of teachers' and students' voices. Relatedness is all about teachers fostering awareness and unconditional acceptance of both themselves and their students.

From MBT's Studio

Teenager Anne-Marie often has difficulty in seeing her own success because she has a keen eye for recognizing her own shortcomings. So, if she doesn't get as far with her studies as she planned, she wastes no time in sharing that information with me. As she moves through her high school years, it seems likely emotional pressures and physical instability will contribute to the way she critically views herself.

During her lessons, my plan is twofold: to listen to her concerns and to provide her with a set of appreciative eyes. This means stepping back from her intensely close view. Opening up spaces at regular intervals to appreciate that while she's so focused on getting things right, there's something uplifting about her musical involvement. Something that may be difficult for her to appreciate given her intensity in the moment. Of course, it's good to be critical. For Anne-Marie, my role is to help keep her criticality in check so she can be uplifted by what music has to offer.

When it comes to relatedness between teachers and students, I like to think my role is much like an experienced and knowledgeable tour guide for my students' lengthy musical journey. As demonstrated in the stories of Chloe and Anne-Marie, I'm responsible for making sure my students get safely from one location to another. I take charge of the direction at times, along with recommendations for outstanding places to visit and places to avoid. However, I'm very much aware that it's the students' musical journey, not mine. Students depend on my ability to guide them, to help them get familiar, and to encourage their own independent explorations at all stages of their journey. It's my job to point out things along their journey that they might miss if I don't point them out.

This means it's important for me to be aware of and acceptant of who my students are: their idiosyncrasies, their personality and character, their musical interests. I need to get to know them not only before the tour begins, but all along the journey through conversations and reflections. It also means that students get to know a great deal about the musical things and ideas that are important to me. After all, the reason for having me as a tour guide is so they won't need to find out everything for themselves. But, if all we're doing is visiting the musical places I like, it's a pretty one-sided tour. Likewise, if all we're doing is visiting students' favorite musical destinations or places they can find on their own, there's not much point to having me as a tour guide.

UNCONDITIONAL PERSONAL CONNECTIONS

As an aspect of relatedness, unconditional personal connections between teachers and students involve illuminating conversations, silences, questioning, and intuitions that occur on a weekly basis. Connecting with students in unconditional and personal ways is something I take seriously. I look fastidiously at student details. How do students enter the room? Do they come with their parents? If so, who enters first? What words do they use to communicate? What does their body language reveal? Where do their eyes go? Are they comfortable with my questions? I'm also attentive to my own actions: how I acknowledge students, the words I use, where I look when I talk, and the kinds of questions I ask. Particularly during a new student's first weeks of lessons, I do everything I can to demonstrate warmth, sincerity, likability, cooperation, and readiness. It's something I do no matter students age or level of playing because I know that students will pick up quickly on who I am and that who we are precedes what we do together. So I'm mindful that my language, gestures, body language, and tone of voice need to be student compatible. I avoid being overly bold with shy students or artificially friendly with self-assured students, and I stay away from the perils of overeagerness like smiling too hard, trying to be too witty, being overly polite, too clever, and patronizing. I want students to feel they can trust me and that I have an immense willingness to be sociable, to accept and care for others, and provide a safe environment for musical explorations.

Your Thoughts

Teachers' language, gestures, body language, and tone of voice impact their ability to make unconditional personal connections with students.

1. What positive aspects come to mind regarding your own teachers' ability to make unconditional personal connections?
2. What might have gotten in the way?
3. What made it possible?

With unconditional and highly personal connections as our mutual starting point, my role as teacher is to actively engage students in musical explorations that are immediate, fun, and attainable. In this respect, safe, trusting, and cooperative interactions are key to providing the foundation for teaching with instant enjoyment and immediate success. This feature of teaching is affirmed in the work of Ithaca College associate professor P. R. Subramaniam who proposed that educators offer activities or tasks that give students ample exploratory opportunities ultimately leading to the instant enjoyment of learning.[3] Subramaniam's emphasis on instant enjoyment is of particular importance with students whose trust in teachers may be meaningfully amplified by the immediacy of their enjoyment and achievement. Conversely, students' belief in teachers' trustworthiness may be severely jeopardized by overly passive and lengthy instructional tasks.

To facilitate instant enjoyment and immediate success with my students, I purposefully break down and expand activities in relation to what students can positively handle. When musical explorations are too difficult, I find something easier. When there's a lack of sufficient challenge, I find ways to explore at a higher level. I favor vocabulary my students can understand and use their experiences to introduce new words or concepts. I ask questions that students may easily answer within their realm of comprehension, avoiding those that may result in "I don't know" as an answer. I often marvel aloud at their ability to answer my inquiries. Above all, I'm fastidious in validating students' success with empowering descriptive language, deliberately stepping away from what might be termed as noncommittal language. By using language to empower students' awareness of their success, it's not unusual for me to follow up successful students' performances with conversations similar to the following:

MBT (smiling): Nicely done! What do you think?

Student (passive): It was good.

MBT (incredulous): Good?? I thought it was fantastic! Why don't you play it again and we'll check it out. (Student successfully plays again.) Yes! It definitely was fantastic. What do you think?

Student (hesitating): It was fantastic?

MBT (championing): Absolutely! Or if you want, you could even say amazing! Or extraordinary! How about best ever!

Student (active): Okay. Amazing!

My goal isn't merely to help students be successful. It's to make sure students actually enjoy their success, that they're uplifted by what they accomplish. For all levels, but especially beginners, I encourage this kind of active affirmative language, knowing that when they get home, students are more likely to be interested in reengaging with "amazing" or "fantastic" explorations than "good" ones. Not to mention, it'll be a lot of fun to reexamine their "fantastic" explorations at their next lesson. Also, at the end of their lessons, in making notes for homework, I ask them to guide me with their insights into our explorations as another opportunity to point out their successes and reinforce the enjoyment that comes with musical explorations.

Teaching Tip

√ Uplift students' musical journeys.

1. Help students see what they can't see.
2. Help students work through the mismatch between vulnerability and confidence.

Taking on the role of a generous musical tour guide may explain a lot about why I enjoy teaching so much, because every week I have the privilege of highlighting my students' successes and enjoyment. Through the marvels of musical exploration, I get to see students experiencing themselves as dynamic and aware individuals. And because we participate in an ongoing unconditional and personal connection, I'm frequently grateful for what my students' awareness might shed light on. For example, after ten years of hosting my student André on a weekly basis, the following conversation took place when I asked him to share his thoughts.

From MBT's Studio

"What would you say is the one thing you're most interested in?" I inquired. There was momentary silence as fifteen-year-old André scanned the room, as if somehow his eyes could sum up his thoughts. "Freedom," he replied. Not sure where he was going, I prompted, "Freedom to . . . ?" Without missing a beat André continued, "Freedom to be the person I really am." Hoping I might round out his insight, I added, "Rather than the person everyone else thinks you should be." André nodded his head in agreement.

André's interest in freedom serves as a precious reminder that music teaching requires inclusive and sensitive teachers who understand and appreciate their students, who safely engage their enjoyment and success. Music teaching calls upon teachers who interact without hesitation because they're comfortable with our human mismatch of vulnerability and self-confidence. Through the weekly routine of uncharted yet unconditional personal connections, music teachers may establish dynamic and desirable conditions for relatedness with their students.

THE POWER OF SMILING

There may be no better way for teachers to set the tone of their relatedness with students than by smiling. Even before teachers find out about their students or respond to questions, before handing out studio policies or tuition documents, smiling reveals a lot about what students might expect from their teachers. It tells them that teachers care about their students and strive to create educational spaces where students feel a sense of safety, inclusion, and value. Smiling is an easy way for teachers to show sensitivity to their students' vulnerability and support their most basic needs of acceptance and belonging before engaging with the business of learning. Smiling helps teachers to build their essential social/relational connection with students as the precursor to triggering and holding onto students' interest.

Your Thoughts
Smiling.

1. How often do you think you smile while teaching?
2. What might be holding you back?
3. What makes genuine smiling possible?

When we smile, we initiate an entire flush of extraordinary changes to our outlook because facial expressions not only communicate our current mood, they also have the ability to influence our mood as well. Studies by P. B. Pillippen revealed that smiling has a positive impact on numerous physical, subconscious, intellectual, and emotional levels.[4] Smiling calms the heart and relaxes the body. It reduces blood pressure and lets us physically work without overworking. In counteracting the stresses associated with unfamiliar situations, smiling helps in broadening and opening our perceptions to insights that might come from our own or another person's subconscious. By choosing to smile, we can bring about positive internal and external changes that automatically impact our capacity for creativity, learning, and decision-making.

Teaching Tip

√ Smile and the whole world smiles with you.

1. Smile with your words and tone of voice.
2. Smile with your eyes.
3. Watch for students' smiles and/or lack of smiles.

The anatomy of smiling is captured in the curls at the corners of the mouth, in the twinkle of the eyes, and in the way a person tilts and nods their head. These multilayered dynamics of facial expression essentially transmit a snapshot of information that others may interpret. By contracting or expanding the muscles of our face in different degrees and combinations, we provide clues to our emotional and mental state, our well-being and personality, our physical health. Whether we smile intentionally or not, smiles carry a consistent message across cultures of approachability, friendliness, and how we feel about our immediate environment.

From MBT's Studio

When my fourteen-year-old student Jordan arrives for a lesson without a smile on his face, I know that we'll need a more relaxed pace. It may mean that we'll not talk as much as usual. I might want to ask, "Anything I should know about?" Then again, maybe it's not a good day to ask for more information.

When my six-year-old student Danielle arrives for a lesson without a smile on her face, I know that she'll appreciate it when we take time to breathe deeply between pieces. She'll feel better after we get up and walk around the bench a couple of times. A couple of stretches with eyes closed may be useful.

By the end of their lessons, perhaps a smile will have found its way onto their faces. It's not a requirement, but when it happens, I'm grateful.

In working with my own students, smiling has two important relatedness implications. First, I smile to communicate my own approachability, courteousness, credibility, and competency. I want students to be comfortable with the immediacy of our relationship. Second, I interpret students' smiles as an indication of how they feel about what's going on. Given that lesson activities involve all kinds of intensities, students' smiles may reveal whether they're fully engaged, passively taking part, or completely disconnected from what we're doing together. This doesn't mean my teaching is only about encouraging students to smile. Obviously, there are numerous occasions when not smiling may be an indication of complete engagement. Paying attention to my students' facial expressions helps me stay attuned to their state of mind. The information gleaned from the intensity of their smiles or lack of them, lets me know when it might be appropriate and how it might be beneficial to introduce a bit of humor—a momentary indulgence in lightheartedness.

SENSE OF HUMOR

This aspect of relatedness may be characterized as the capacity we have for taking delight in the extraordinary and ordinary situations of life. Humor is experienced in those moments of optimistic amusement that often arrive unpredictably as demonstrated in the following example from my teaching:

From MBT's Studio

Nathan's performance confidently displayed his own refreshing approach to dynamics. "I could hear your imagination going full force all the way through," I enthusiastically reported. "I'll bet people are always telling you what a great imagination you have."

"Well," Nathan affirmed nonchalantly, "actually, some of my friends have said I do have a good *imagi-Nathan!*"

Humorous incidents like Nathan's *imagi-Nathan* have vital implications for teaching and learning because they strengthen the connection between students and teachers. They emphasize how students' and teachers' shared amusement can reinforce their relationship. As a highly widespread and appealing social phenomenon, humor is deeply embedded in culture, personal attitudes, interpersonal structures, and current trends. Whether it's a joke, riddle, anecdote, or one-liner, humor most typically occurs as the result of an obvious yet desirable mismatch between what we expect to occur and what actually occurs. According to Johns Hopkins University professor Ronald A. Berk, a self-identified humor enthusiast, most forms of humor incorporate incongruity, that is, the "juxtaposition of the expected with the unexpected."[5] We might even describe humor as taking pleasure in those delightful moments when predictability and routine are replaced by something comical, something that elicits our laughter and tugs at our sense of enjoyment. Humor is about our ability to discover, express, and appreciate what's funny about the twists of life. Humor invites us to be taken by surprise, to welcome the absurd and ludicrous. It champions our optimism and amusement in the illogical, exaggerated, unreasonable, inappropriate, and unexpected.

Your Thoughts

Humor is a great way to strengthen connections between teachers and students.

1. Which of your students likes to tell jokes? Why?
2. How do you feel about using humor as a teaching strategy?

Education scholar Mary Kay Morrison has researched the use of humor to maximize learning. Morrison's work is noteworthy in pointing out how the element of surprise in humor "defies the brain's predictions and expectations. When someone acts out of the ordinary, when something unusual happens, our brain pays attention."[6] Using humor is an effective teaching strategy because it attracts students' attention and interrupts their awareness, therein increasing their active comprehension, retention, interest, and performance. By promoting creativity and encouraging divergent thought processes, humor may help students overcome resistance to learning routines, provide temporary relief from overexertion, and introduce playfulness as a way to express the truth even when it might be hard to take. Humor often succeeds where other methods have failed.

Using humor as a teaching tool is always context-bound. It depends on the student's age level, the content of instruction, and the immediacy of understanding. For teachers, it's not enough to merely attract students' attention or interrupt their awareness through humor. As American University professor R. L. Garner describes, for humor to be most effective in learning situations, it must be "specific, targeted, and appropriate to the subject matter."[7] Not all teachers are comfortable with using humor in educational settings. Some believe their role as teachers and their subject are too serious to merit using humor. They view humor as a disservice to the gravity of teaching and learning, appropriate only outside the boundaries of educational interaction. For other teachers, their use of humor is directed at maximizing their comedic finesse. They obsessively inject humor at every instructional opportunity. With little or nonexistent connection to students or the topic of exploration, they teach with an endless stream of jokes, one-liners, riddles, or anecdotes designed to entertain but lack in educational value. When properly used, humor may effectively make learning more enjoyable and sustain a meaningful learning environment without trivializing the opportunity for intentional learning or falling into the pitfalls associated with overzealous teacher comedians.

Teaching Tip

√ Keep humor close at hand. Laugh when you can.

1. Keep humor simple.
2. Keep playfulness in context.

I appreciate using humor in my own teaching because of how it keeps me attentive to students' moods and how it strengthens their involvement in learning. My goal is to incorporate humor in age-sensitive and individually suitable ways because humor for a sixteen-year-old is not the same for a seven-year old; nor is it humorous to incessantly bring up Nathan's *imagina-Nathan*. Humor does have limitations. As a consequence, I tend to keep things simple, relying on twists of language that convey exaggeration and surprise in order to elicit students' response. I treat humor as a two-way street, wherein it's marvelous to watch for students' response and to delight in their own spontaneous, humorous injections. It can be great fun for both of us to use deliberate over- and under-statements to talk about tone production, technique, interpretation, and rhythmic continuity. For example, with beginners, we might better describe stiff fingers as the "best poking fingers" we've ever seen. My goal is to teach with straightforward words that have life to them, words that encourage students to experience their learning with anticipation. It's about using humor to exploit students' exploration of the unexpected—whether fact, thought, feeling, or event.

CARING RELATIONSHIPS

Earlier in *More Than Music Lessons*, I pointed out how there's a universal feeling that people want to be valued for who they are and what they do. Teachers appreciate being valued by students and parents. Likewise, students appreciate being recognized and accepted by their teachers. We all want to experience relationships as worthwhile and life affirming.

Educational research scholars have discussed the impact of caring relationships on students' learning. According to Julia Thompson, the most powerful device available to teachers who want to foster a "favorable learning climate is [to have] a positive relationship with our students."[8] Lee and Marlene Canter remind us that we can all recall, as students, classes in which we did not try very hard because we didn't like our teachers.[9] In contrast, we most likely can also recall classes in which we did try our best, simply because of the positive relationship we had with our teachers. Janet Groen and Colleen Kawalilak also affirm how relatedness in learning is about our human need for care, compassion, inclusion, ethical practice, and community.[10]

Teaching Tip

√ Make caring relationships the trusting
backdrop for good and bad news.

1. Listen with empathy and understanding.
2. Advocate for honest reflection and genuine follow-up.
3. Celebrate achievements and support setbacks.

This chapter has delved into various aspects associated with positive instructional relationships: awareness and acceptance of teachers and students, novelty, smiling, and humor. While these characteristics may contribute to positive relations, it's easy for a positive learning environment to be mistaken as one without discomfort or tension where teachers only say upbeat things about their students and never point out their shortcomings or errors, where there's no failure or frustration. Positive and caring relationships provide the trusting backdrop for teachers to deliver both good and bad news, to deal with difficult subjects that may require teachers' empathy and understanding more than authority or discipline. This means teachers understand the difference between respectful and disrespectful actions, between honest and shaming language, between fostering and destructive interactions. Caring relationships mean teachers advocate for their students in a way that spans a trajectory from supportive to stimulating and acceptant to critical. They promote honest and genuine reflective processes. In this way, teachers make it possible for students to become equally accomplished not only in doing what's easy, but also in handling the problems, complexities, and difficulties associated with learning to sing or play a musical instrument.

Your Thoughts

Caring relationships form the trusting backdrop for good and bad news.

What is your response to this statement?

FAQs

Q: As a teacher, I'm concerned about the relationships I develop with my students. My challenge is that I see two extremes of teaching style. On one side, teachers who want to be their students' friends. On the other, teachers who position themselves on some kind of ivory tower. Can you tell me about what I might find between these two extremes?

A: To get a sense of what's possible between these two extremes, I appreciate the work of Stephen Brookfield in his 2006 book *The Skillful Teacher*.[11] Brookfield is a university researcher who asked students to identify what they considered to be the most important attributes for teachers.

Students' responses highlighted two fundamental teacher qualities: personal authenticity and subject knowledge. Students wanted instructors who were true to themselves; teachers who show up in the classroom as real people, not fake teacher versions or impersonators acting on impressions of what they think others might want teachers to look or sound like. A genuine person with real-life experiences.

Students also wanted instructors who were knowledgeable of their subject matter. Teachers who know what they're talking about through their own experience, not borrowed knowledge or superficial understanding. Educators with real, bonafide knowledge. Both aspects—personal authenticity and subject knowledge—were considered to be essential. Without subject knowledge, personal authenticity was insufficient. Likewise, without personal authenticity, subject knowledge was incomplete. It was the combination of authenticity and knowledge that made students feel confident they could rely on their instructors.

What this research reveals is that there's potential for a lot of variation to teachers' relationships with students that falls between the above extremes. We have many more options and variants than the "friend" relationship or the "ivory tower" teacher might offer.

Build On and Exercise What's Already There

Relatedness: the need to feel that our personal efforts or pursuits are socially connected/integrated.

1. How do you feel about teachers having awareness and acceptance of their students?

2. As a teacher, how do you feel about having awareness and acceptance of yourself?

3. How does your awareness and acceptance of students impact your ability to build on and exercise what's already there?

NOTES

1. Edward Deci and Richard Ryan, *Handbook of Self-determination Research* (Rochester, NY: University of Rochester Press, 2002).

2. Carl Rogers and H. Jerome Freiberg, *Freedom to Learn*, third edition (New York: Macmillan College Publishing Company, 1994).

3. P. R. Subramaniam, "Unlocking the Power of Situational Interest in Physical Education," *Journal of Physical Education, Recreation, & Dance*, 81 no. 7 (2010).

4. P. B. Phillippen, "The Effects of Smiling and Frowning on Perceived Affect and Exertion while Physically Active," *Journal of Sport Behavior*, 35 no. 3 (2012): 337–53.

5. Ronald A. Berk, *Professors Are from Mars and Students Are from Snickers* (Sterling: Stylus, 2003), 11.

6. Mary Kay Morrison, *Using Humor to Maximize Learning: The Links Between Positive Emotions and Education* (Lanham, MD: Rowman & Littlefield, 2010), 50.

7. R. L. Garner, "Humour in Pedagogy: How Ha-ha can Lead to Aha," *College Teaching* 54 no. 1 (2006).

8. Julia Thompson, *Discipline Survival Kit for the Secondary Teacher* (West Nyack, NY: The Center for Applied Research in Education, 1998).

9. Lee Canter and Marlene Canter, *Lee Canter's Assertive Discipline: Positive Behaviour Management for Today's Classroom* (Santa Monica, CA: Lee Canter and Associates, 1997).

10. Janet Groen and Colleen Kawalilak, *Pathways of Adult Learning* (Toronto, ON: Canadian Scholar's Press, 2014).

11. Stephen Brookfield, *The Skillful Teacher: On Technique, Trust, and Responsiveness in the Classroom*, second edition (Hoboken, NJ: Jossey-Bass, 2006).

Chapter 10

Practicing and Reflection

Reflection is the need to consider how our personal efforts or pursuits contribute to and detract from our own lives; the need to critically question and examine our personal efforts and pursuits.

From MBT's Studio

Joanna was a six-year-old student who, according to her mother, could often be quite bossy at home. On many occasions, I began her lessons by saying, "Okay, you be the teacher. Do what you need to do to help me out." Suddenly, I'd thrust my elbow away from my body and I'd look to Joanna for assistance. Gradually, she'd guide my elbow back to its appropriate place. Then, I'd tip my head to the side, or raise my shoulders awkwardly high. I'd look to Joanna for assistance, and each time she'd help me out, until finally, I'd say something like, "Why not just show me how everything needs to be done." In the blink of an eye, Joanna would set herself up on the piano chair and launch herself into a performance with everything that needed to be done. By all accounts, Joanna was an astute observer, directly effective teacher, and a champion of demonstration.

At a workshop for intermediate students between the ages of twelve and fourteen, I begin by getting to know the students' names. As everyone seems comfortable, I think it would be interesting to explore their reflective thinking processes. I casually ask, "How do you know if you're playing a piece well or not?" With most students playing for more than six years, I expect them to respond with answers that emphasize things like "looking at the musical score" or "checking the metronome marking" or "pay attention to the dynamics." However, not one student mentions anything like that.

Instead, the students suggest, "When my teacher tells me." Hearing the students' honest response was like a giant alarm bell going off, reminding me how easy it is for teacher guidance to turn into student dependence. On the one hand,

I recognize teachers' feedback for students can be a good thing. On the other, total reliance on teachers' feedback can result in students being deprived of their own reflective thinking.

These stories illustrate how reflective processes may and may not take shape. In Joanna's story, I put myself in the role of student to capitalize on her desire to take charge, therein confirming her ability to think things through. It's amazing to watch as she turns her reflective process into action. In the piano workshop, we see something quite different—students whose reflective processes have been overshadowed by their teachers' good intentions. For them, the answer to "How do you know when you're playing a piece well or not?" remains a mystery that can only be solved by the teacher's expertise. Unfortunately, students' own reflective capacity continues untapped and undeveloped.

Reflection refers to our basic need to figure out what's working and what's not working, our need to evaluate what happens when we apply our skills and knowledge to a given context. Reflection may occur spontaneously in the split-second example of a person removing their hand from contact with a burning hot object. It may also involve prolonged processes wherein a person makes connections between pieces of knowledge, like the itch of a mosquito bite and its subsequent inflamed swelling. Without reflection, we may find ourselves caught in perpetual loops of unnecessarily burning ourselves and aggravating inflammations. Reflection helps in identifying when to keep on doing what we're doing, when to try a different approach, and when it might be most advantageous to seek help from others.

I appreciate how researchers Arthur Costa and Bena Kallick use the word metacognition to describe how people plan for, reflect on, and evaluate the quality of their own thinking skills and strategies.[1] In their interpretation, reflection involves multiple layers. It means becoming increasingly aware of one's actions and their effect on others and the environment; forming internal questions in the search for information and meaning; developing plans of action, mentally rehearsing before a performance; monitoring plans as they are employed; reflecting on the completed plan for self-evaluation; and editing for improved performance. The challenge with reflection, as organizational psychologist Adam Grant identifies, is that questioning ourselves makes the world more unpredictable.[2] We favor listening to views that make us feel good instead of ideas that make us think hard. Often, reconsidering something we believe deeply or have worked hard to achieve can threaten our identities making it feel as if we're losing a part of ourselves. In other words, opening our minds to reflection is a complicated and not always easy undertaking.

Your Thoughts

Reflection refers to our need to figure out what's working and what's not working.

1. How would you describe your own experience as a student with reflection?
2. What did your teacher do or not do to encourage your reflective processes?

DEVELOPING AWARENESS

While reflective processes are typically associated with decision-making related to what we might do next, I like to think of reflection as starting with the simple awareness of what we're doing right now. Before we can make any decisions regarding further performance or exploration, we need to be able to recognize what we're currently doing. This means that before students can begin honing their skills as reflective thinkers, they need to engage their skills of musical observation. That's why, especially with elementary-level students, I spend a lot of time reinforcing their awareness of various musical aspects and the language we use to talk about musical performance.

To tap into students' observation skills and develop their familiarity with musical vocabulary, I pay close attention to three fundamental instructional themes: demonstration, description, and opposites. 1. Demonstration. I provide musical demonstrations so that students can see and hear actual examples of musical performance. I invite students' own demonstrations as confirmation of their musical understanding. I want students to be actively involved in their own musical explorations. 2. Description. I use descriptive and nonjudgmental language to convey important information regarding students' performances and my demonstrations. I encourage students' use of a musical vocabulary and invite them to share their own observations so that our communication benefits from the combination of teacher and student input. 3. Opposites. I strengthen students' musical awareness by exploring opposite perspectives, such as the contrast between stiff and flexible fingers, deep and light tone, staccato and legato touch. The following scenario provides an example of how demonstration, description, and opposites may contribute to a safe and supportive lesson environment.

An elementary student plays with inconsistent legato touch, that is, several random staccato notes.

Teacher: "Thanks so much. Now, I'm going to play two times. One time with no jumping notes at all. One time with some jumping notes. See if you can tell which is which." Teacher performs as described.

Teacher: "Which had the jumping notes and which one didn't?"

Student: "Number one had jumping notes and number two didn't."

Teacher: "That's right. I'm curious to see if you can play with some jumping notes." Student performs with some jumping notes.

Teacher: "Tell me what you did."

Student: "I played with jumping notes."

Teacher: "What about no jumping notes?"

Student performs with no jumping notes.

Teacher: "Tell me what you did that time."

Student: "I played with no jumping notes. They're all sticky."

Teacher: "At home, have fun playing with no jumping or sticky notes as much as you can. And to keep things interesting, why not throw in a couple of jumping notes if you like."

In terms of demonstration, we see how the teacher provides a secure model for the student's observation, and how the student's demonstration confirms their understanding and performance skill. The teacher's demonstration serves as a launchpad for the student's autonomy and active participation in their own learning. While the above example showcases an elementary-level piano student, demonstration, description, and opposites provide a practical framework for students at all levels—including advanced students. Likewise, vocal and non-keyboard instructors may also use the above formula to target voice-specific and instrument-specific aspects as appropriate to students' musical development.

By using descriptive language, the teacher gives pertinent feedback to the student without labeling the inconsistencies in performance as bad or wrong. Professors of education John Hattie and Helen Timperley at the University of Auckland point out that teacher feedback on how students specifically perform a task is actually much more helpful than praise.[3] However, using descriptive language shouldn't be misinterpreted as substituting "no jumping" for "legato." It's about using descriptions to provide students with accurate information about what they've done, rather than teachers dogmatically imposing or monitoring what students should do. Descriptive language is honest and truthful, not controlling or degrading. Furthermore, in the above scenario the student's response of "sticky" notes not only confirms understanding but also provides the teacher with language to support home practice. Through speaking and performing, the student is able to communicate with and learn from the teacher.

Exploration of opposites heightens student's musical awareness because differentiating between legato and staccato stimulates the multilayered engagement of student's mind and body. For Swiss cellist Thomas Demenga, this means that students shouldn't necessarily practice a passage over and over again in a single, uniform way. They should try out many different and even musically "wrong" versions in order to develop a freer attitude to performance.[4] Counterstrategies, like exploring opposites, may work with amazing efficiency because they give students permission to take manageable risks and be creative. Opposites remind us that musical development doesn't take place within a singular context or approach. By moving explorations outside the predictable and comfortable, students not only develop listening and performing capacities, they also learn to trust their own musicianship in multiple situations.

Finally, the teacher's closing remarks are significant. Knowing that the student would most likely encounter a certain amount of performance inconsistency during the coming week, the teacher suggests incorporating large amounts of legato and small amounts of staccato as a way of stimulating consistency in student awareness.

Teaching Tip

√ Stimulate, strengthen, and maintain students' awareness necessary for reflective thinking.

1. Incorporate teacher and student demonstrations.
2. Allow for teacher and student descriptions.
3. Explore opposites as appropriate.

Throughout the lengthy process of students' musical development, the strategies of demonstration, description, and opposites naturally incorporate instrument-specific, student age- and level-appropriate considerations, not to mention the student's own personality traits. Ultimately, what's important is that teachers help students to strengthen, stimulate, and maintain the awareness necessary for reflective thinking. Teachers assist students in learning how to give feedback to themselves. They create opportunities for students to consider what to do next by starting with what they're currently doing.

QUESTIONS

Asking good questions may be one of the most effective ways for teachers to guide the development of students' reflective thinking. Teachers ask questions to find out what students know and how they use their knowledge to inform understanding. They ask students to analyze their performances, to take things apart, and put them back together again. Asking good, reflective questions may require considerable teaching skill in orchestrating the words, phrases, nuances, and intonations appropriate to the idea, student, and moment.

According to educational author Selma Wasserman, the art of questioning is much more than making interrogative demands.[5] Wasserman believes that if questions are to bear fruit, then questioning must be sensitive to other aspects of any interrogative process. These include an awareness of how questions are framed and how they may provoke anxiety, thereby influencing the nature of students' responses. Good questions are clear in what they're asking students to think about and not broad or abstract so they defeat the process of thoughtful examination. Good questions invite, not command, students to think reflectively. They build trust in the interactive and respectful relationship between teacher and student.

I typically approach question-and-answer activities with one overarching principle: ask questions in a way that students are able to answer them. To illustrate, take a look at the following two scenarios:

Scenario 1: Midway through a junior-level student's lesson the teacher says, "Okay now, play *The Waltz.*" The student plays the selection from memory. The teacher asks, "What did you notice in your performance?" The student says, "I'm not sure . . . " The teacher says helpfully, "What about your memory? How about keeping the beat? Is there any place you sped up?" The student says, "I think it was okay . . . " The teacher says, "What was okay? Your memory? Or the beat?" The student says, "I think the beat was okay. Maybe not. I'm not sure."

Scenario 2: Midway through a junior-level student's lesson the teacher says, "Okay now, play *The Waltz.* Let's check your memory and consistency with the beat this time around." The student plays the selection from memory. The teacher asks, "What did you notice about your memory?" The student says, "I still have that spot in line 3." The teacher asks, "Can you show me where?" The student points to the bar in the score. The teacher says, "I see. . . . How about the beat? Is there any place you sped up?" The student says, "I think I sped up, but I can't tell where it is."

Both teachers share remarkable similarities in being sensitive to the student's process of reflective thinking. Perhaps teachers are aware students may have a history of discomfort with questions, so they introduce reflections midway through the lesson, allowing the student to get comfortable with their interactive relationship. When the Scenario 1 student struggles to answer the first question, the teacher kindly responds by posing questions that could potentially lead the student to various solutions. Yet the variety of questions and potential answers only leads to further student indecision. There's an unmistakable feeling from the outset of the student's reply, "I'm not sure . . . " that the teacher will be hard-pressed to stimulate student confidence as a reflective thinker. Thus, the Scenario 1 student's history of discomfort with questions most likely continues unchanged. In contrast, the teacher in Scenario 2 curtails the history of discomfort with questions by introducing the reflective process before rather than after the student's performance. The teacher follows up with one question at a time to avoid overloading the student's reflective thinking. When the Scenario 2 student replies, "I can't tell where . . . ," there's a sense that student and teacher can work together to resolve student indecision all because the teacher initiated the reflective process prior to performance rather than after.

The above scenarios illustrate how teachers may differ by taking reactive and proactive approaches to developing reflective thinking. While teachers in both scenarios work from an understanding of students, practical experience of music, and knowledge of teaching, they teach students from different perspectives. On the reactive teaching side, the teacher in Scenario 1 responds spontaneously to the issues displayed in the student's performance. The teacher's follow-up with reflective questioning comes directly from the immediacy of having heard the student perform, but fails to generate any recognizable growth in the student's reflective process.

Whereas on the proactive teaching side, the teacher in Scenario 2 works with a plan of action that supports students' reflective thinking in relation to what students have previously done, what they're doing right now, and what teachers envision for their students' futures. Proactive teachers are able to introduce reflective processes prior to student's performance because they anticipate how their students will prepare their repertoire—they know how certain students will excel in memorizing but not in keeping the beat, how other students will excel in dynamic expression but not in following advantageous fingerings. Proactive teachers also know the challenges that come with particular repertoire selections. And they're willing to ask questions in ways that students are able to answer. Furthermore, because teachers are familiar with students' previous responses to questions, they may present question/answer routines that synchronize with their students' preferred way of answering questions. Not all questions need to be answered on the spot and some students may benefit from an adjusted time line. Students may appreciate having time to put together their thoughts at home before next week's lesson. Others may value the opportunity to organize their response on paper, choosing a written rather than verbal summary.

Teaching Tip

√ Be proactive instead of reactive when it comes to questions.

1. Start with questions the student can answer.
2. Ask one question at a time.
3. Work collaboratively to resolve student indecision.

The problem with the difference between reactive and proactive processes is that many teachers may think they're proactively getting students accustomed to reflective thinking, when they're actually using reactive processes that leave students feeling misunderstood. Teachers who instruct similarly to Scenario 1 may think that they're doing their best to develop reflective thinking even when students fail to answer questions and that it's really not their fault if students can't answer their questions. This means that before teachers can expect students to function as confident, reflective thinkers, teachers may need to examine their own experience with using reactive and proactive processes and critically consider how such processes genuinely impact the student's current participation in reflective thinking.

SILENCE

During the 1970s, University of Florida science educator Mary Budd Rowe (1925–1996) conducted a six-year research project that studied teachers asking questions of their students. Specifically, Rowe measured the period of silence that followed teachers' questions. She found, on average, that silence rarely

Practicing and Reflection

lasted more than 1.5 seconds in typical teacher/student interactions across a wide variety of instructional situations and levels, ranging from elementary schools to university settings, from classrooms to museums and business settings. Most teachers waited less than one second for students to answer a question.[6]

Your Thoughts

How comfortable are you with silence?

Take an informal examination of how long you wait for students to answer your questions. You may be surprised.

Rowe's research is significant in the way it sheds light on how teachers may be uncomfortable with silence. It's as if teachers assume that silence is the undesirable indication of students not knowing the answer to questions. Teachers may presume that quickly answered questions are a sign of students' purposeful engagement with learning. Yet when we think about it, quick answers may not be all that desirable because they're most likely the result of students memorizing information or only tapping into surface materials. In order for students to engage in deep thinking, reflective processing, or analysis, teachers may need to slow down the timing of question-and-answer activities. They may need to get comfortable with silence.

Teaching Tip

√ Get comfortable with silence.

1. Give students ample time to think.
2. Provide guidance as necessary.
3. Be patient.

In my own teaching, I've become comfortable with allowing for silence as the necessary requirement for answering reflective questions, encouraging my students to be generous with their own thinking processes. Reflective questions can take anywhere from fifteen to thirty seconds to answer, maybe even longer on occasion. Often with teenagers who may seem perpetually annoyed with any kind of question, I reassure them with statements like, "Don't rush your thinking. I have great confidence in your ability to think this through." Thus, by setting up students for answering questions and by allowing them time for reflection, my intention is to find out more about my students and how they think in a safe and supportive environment.

FOLLOW-UP

One additional condition related to reflective thinking is the teacher's ability to resist the temptation to always follow-up with evaluative statements like, "Good idea" or "That's an interesting thought" or "Not quite." Although evaluation is an important component of teaching and learning processes, evaluation may also shut down students' reflective thinking rather than facilitate it. For example, there's considerable difference between "That's right" or "That's wrong" and "Thanks for sharing your thoughts."

To avoid getting caught in a predictable pattern of evaluating my students' responses, I might repeat the idea back to the student or try to paraphrase their statements without taking credit for their thoughts. I encourage students to push the boundaries of their reflective thinking by asking for more information, saying something like, "Tell me more about what you mean" or "Where does that idea come from?" Above all, I want to affirm students' ownership of their own thoughts and to let them know that I appreciate their efforts. I frequently use statements like, "I see," "I get what you're saying," and "Thank you" because such expressions can go a long way in supporting students as reflective thinkers.

Teaching Tip

√ Follow-up students' reflection with affirmation, inquiry, and appreciation.

1. I see where you're going.
2. Tell more about it.
3. Thanks for sharing.

STUDENT REPORT CARDS

When I first started keeping student report cards, I did so because I wanted to keep track of my students' progress. I appreciated how student report cards are a practical solution, because with fifty or more students in my studio, it is virtually impossible for me to keep an accurate image of each student over long periods of time. What I never anticipated was that student report cards would also provide a practical means for monitoring consistencies and inconsistencies in my teaching. Because I keep previous and current student report cards, I can get both long- and short-term perspectives of what's working and what needs extra attention or a different approach. I can

Table 10.1.

Piano Studio of Dr. Merlin B. Thompson		
Student Name:		Date of Birth:
Start Date:	Current Level:	Current Level:
	December	June
Study Habits		
Technical Development		
Reading Development		
Self Expression		
Attitude		
Events Attended		
General Progress		
Life Skills		
Family Home Life		

adjust my teaching at the individual student's level and for entire groups of students in my studio.

Table 10.1 illustrates the format I use for all levels of students. After reviewing an individual student's report cards from previous years, I fill out the current sections. I find it useful to look back at previous report cards to get a sense of students' progress. For all levels of students, I typically select the most appropriate from: "Excellent," "Satisfactory," "Coming Along," and "Needs Work." When more information is necessary, I include a single descriptive sentence.

I appreciate how student report cards offer a snapshot of students' progress that differs from their weekly lessons. By looking back to previous years and comparing with students' current status, I can see where they may be experiencing a slowdown and where their progress continues smoothly. I can identify strengths and weaknesses in my own teaching. On occasion, student

Teaching Tip

√ Use student report cards to track student progress and teacher effectiveness.

1. Include pertinent information.
2. Refer to previous year's student report cards.
3. Adjust as necessary.

report cards provide the professional encouragement I might need to reach out to a colleague for ideas, or consult the internet to obtain resources from other music teachers. I also appreciate how looking back at several years of report cards may provide further insight into what's going on in my studio.

PARENT CHECK-INS

From MBT's Studio

During my early years of teaching, a conversation with my mom, Eva Thompson, had an amazing outcome. It took place at a time when the topic of parents was significantly on my mind. Curious to know how she and my dad had managed to successfully raise four children, I asked, "Did you read Dr. Spock's book? How did you know what to do?" She replied, "We had no time to think about anything. The only thing we had time for was doing."

It was a light bulb moment. Knowing that parents were busy with little time for reflection made me wonder what teachers could do to help out. What could I do to provide a space for reflective conversations? What would parents need from me? How would it work? Not long after, I implemented Parent Check-Ins in my studio and the process was underway.

In keeping with making strong connections to students' family home life (see part 1), I incorporate Parent Check-Ins three times a year, during the months of September, January, and June. I use this strategy primarily while students are under thirteen years of age. Approximately one week prior to meeting with parents, I send an email asking them to casually explore three topics with their child: musical goals, life skills, and family home life (an example of the Parent Letter is available in appendix B). I typically spend fifteen minutes of discussion with parents either in my studio or online. As students usually want to be included, I give them a quick hello before sending them out of my studio so I may talk privately with their parents.

With September as the start of our school year, it's a great time to initiate thinking about what might be possible in the coming months. January is the midpoint of the school year, so we shift focus to consider what has happened thus far and what adjustments may be productive. June is the end of the school year—a time to reflect and consider what worked and what didn't. When next September rolls around, we have a good idea of how we might continue to build on the previous year.

Musical goals, life skills, and family home life form the framework for Parent Check-Ins discussions. By including these topics in our discussions, I hope to make it clear that students' musical achievements aren't something separate from their family home life and who they are. These factors overlap and intersect in ways that may stimulate and impede students' musical development. Therefore, it's important to meaningfully reflect on this dynamic combination.

Teaching Tip

√ Use Parent Check-Ins to strengthen connections to students' family home life.

1. Encourage parents to gather information.
2. Listen to what parents have to share.
3. Keep parents in the loop.

During Parent Check-Ins, I appreciate the opportunity to listen to what parents have to say and to share with them my own reflections from the student report cards. Most often, it's interesting to see the direct connection between parents' thoughts and the report cards. It's a great way to reinforce that parents and teacher both have something to contribute to students' ongoing development. On many occasions, parents express their appreciation for being included in this way.

My goal is to create an environment of openness and reciprocal trust where it's not about rolling out my own agenda, nor parents running the show. It's about listening to each other for the student's benefit. My responsibility to students and parents is to welcome them into meaningful, ongoing reflective processes.

TEEN STUDENT REVIEWS

For students fourteen years of age and older, I incorporate Teen Student Reviews during the months of September, January, and June. Approximately one week prior to this event, I send students an email asking them to explore three topics: musical goals, life skills, and their own non-performance music project (an example of the Teen Letter is available in appendix B). I also complete student report cards to share with them. The purpose of Teen Student Reviews is to assist with planning, reflecting, and fine-tuning students' musical journey. I allow five to ten minutes time during their lesson for our discussions. I keep parents in the loop with a conversation over the telephone.

Teaching Tip

√ Use Teen Student Reviews to plan, reflect, and fine-tune students' musical journey.

1. Put students in charge of gathering information.
2. Listen to what students have to share.
3. Ask students for questions.

FAQs

Q: Recently, I tried to be proactive by introducing my student to reflective thinking before her performance rather than after. However, when I asked her a question after her performance, she still answered, "I'm not sure." Just like always. Does being proactive really work?

A: The difficulty all teachers face in modifying their instructional approach is that students have most likely grown accustomed to interacting with their teachers in certain ways. So, even though the teacher tries using a proactive approach, the student doesn't notice the change in approach and continues to respond using the most familiar pattern.

Fortunately, teachers are capable of assisting students with change. For example, at a master class workshop I taught in California, after the home teacher informed me about her very reserved student, I did everything I could to put the student at ease during her lesson. I slowed down my approach. I took my time and waited for eye contact. I smiled and asked questions I knew she could answer like, "Had she visited Canada?" "What about the weather outside?" I opened up space for her to talk. I asked questions in a way that I knew she'd be comfortable with so that when it came time to talk about music, we'd already established how we would interact with each other.

All in all, we had quite a fruitful discussion and I was encouraged to think that the reserved student might be less reserved in her next lesson. That is until moments later when I heard the home teacher say to her student, "Well, it's nice to see you actually have something to say."

Sometimes, what's most crucial in effective interactions with students is for teachers to abandon out-of-date and inaccurate preconceptions of who students are. Starting afresh may have immensely positive results. Giving students time to think at home and allowing for written responses may also prove beneficial.

Q: I currently have a class of forty-five students. How much time will it take to complete forty-five student report cards?

A: Making student report cards doesn't need to take an unreasonable amount of time. Generally speaking, completing them goes fairly quickly as I'm typically only choosing from "Excellent," "Satisfactory," "Coming Along," "Needs Work," or limiting my response to a single descriptive sentence. Using the computer, I may complete each report card in no more than a couple of minutes. Completing fifty shouldn't take more than two to three hours in total. What's key is that they are a starting point for discussions with parents and a record for my own instructional reflection. They need to contain enough information to be useful but not so much that they are onerous for teachers to complete.

Q: How much time do you put aside for Parent Check-Ins? And do you charge for this time period?

A: I include the cost of a fifteen-minute Parent Check-In for each student in the term's tuition based on my hourly instructional rate. I schedule all Parent Check-Ins during one entire week in September, January, and June. I don't teach any student lessons on the weeks of Parent Check-Ins, knowing that parents already have enough to do without making two trips to my studio. Not to mention the impossibility of scheduling fifty Parent Check-Ins in addition to my regular teaching schedule.

Build On and Exercise What's Already There

Reflection is the need to consider how our personal efforts or pursuits contribute to and detract from our own lives. This exploration included: developing awareness, questions, silence, follow-up, student report cards, Parent Check-Ins, and Teen Student Reviews.

1. How do you promote reflective activities with your students? What works? What could you do differently?
2. Student report cards, Parent Check-Ins, and Teen Student Reviews provide opportunities to reflection and sharing. How do you incorporate these strategies in your teaching?

NOTES

1. Arthur Costa and Bena Kallick, *Learning and Leading with Habits of Mind* (Alexandria, VA: ASCD, 2008).
2. Adam Grant, *Think Again* (New York: Viking, 2021).
3. John Hattie and Helen Timperley, "The Power of Feedback," *Review of Educational Research* 77 no. 1 (2007): 81–112.
4. Thomas Demenga, *The Art of Distraction Is More Effective than Repetitive Practice* (February 13, 2014).

5. Selma Wasserman, *Asking the Right Question: The Essence of Teaching* (Bloomington, IN: Phi Beta Kappa Educational Foundation, 1992).

6. Mary Budd Rowe, "Wait Time: Slowing Down May Be a Way of Speeding Up!" *Journal of Teacher Education* 37 no. 1 (1986): 43–50.

Chapter 11

Practicing and Listening

Listening is the need to turn what we hear into what we play. It's the need to transform the sounds in our heads into the sounds we make in performance.

> **From MBT's Studio**
>
> Peter is a fourteen-year-old student who struggled for months to learn an intermediate piano selection. Before beginning another six-page selection of equal difficulty, I suggested, "Peter, why don't you experiment a bit and see how listening to the recording could help you out?" He nodded his head casually like always. However, to my surprise, over the following three weeks he completed the entire second selection section by section. At the third lesson, I asked Peter what he was doing differently, and he replied, "Well, I've been taking my MP3 player to the piano, and I listen to a bit, play a bit. That's all." The strategy worked!

Peter's story provides a simple example of how listening may impact practicing in terms of providing the shortcut for students' successful development. In this final chapter of part 2, I examine multiple ways in which listening is beneficial for learning to sing or play a musical instrument.

Your Thoughts

Thinking back, what role has listening to music played on your own musical development?

LISTENING 001: INTERNALIZE

Listening to music provides a majorly influential spark in learning to sing or play a musical instrument. In Peter's story, listening to the recording allowed him to internalize the second selection's sound as the foundation for his learning process. Being able to hear the piece in his head meant that Peter had what he needed to support his learning explorations. Here, we can see that the influence of listening to repertoire has two distinct benefits. First, it may help students with internalizing various musical aspects before they begin learning the piece. They have an internal advantage in learning their repertoire. Second, it may assist students with progressively refining their repertoire. Listening can help smooth out any number of performance issues for elementary to senior students, from easy to complicated repertoire, from notation to interpretation. For example, my student Jordan's ongoing listening helps to increase his awareness of the distortions that may come from taking the piece apart, practicing hands separately, focusing on fingering, or other details. So, it makes sense for teachers to regularly highlight the benefits that listening to repertoire recordings can bring to students' musical development.

One way that I promote students' awareness of their repertoire listening is by asking them the question, "How does your listening to pieces influence the way you play?" rather than the question, "How much listening to pieces did you do this week?" I'm more interested in supporting the impact of their listening than inquiring into how much they listened because knowing how much they listened doesn't actually provide very useful information. It indicates a quantity or a number but doesn't reveal the effect of listening. Knowing whether their listening had an impact or not sheds light on what we'll do as follow-up. When listening has a positive impact, it makes perfect sense to validate it and keep it in place. When listening has no impact, it's appropriate to figure out what kind of adjustments are possible. Working together, teachers and students can brainstorm to come up with strategies regarding when, where, and specifically what to listen to. Validating my students' listening habits is an important step in their learning to value listening for themselves.

Teaching Tip

√ Listen to promote internalization.

1. Listening to repertoire recordings provides practical learning advantages.

LISTENING 002: INSPIRE

My older brother was the first child in our family to begin piano lessons. Throughout my years in elementary school, I heard him playing the pieces I would eventually learn. Not to mention the performances by my peers and older students I heard at concerts and music festivals. For me, the impact of hearing pieces was inspirational. From John Thompson's "Swans on the Lake" to Joseph Haydn's "Sonata in D major," I simply could not wait to learn the repertoire for myself. Hearing pieces created a magnetic attraction that I couldn't wait to fulfill. What's compelling about this aspect from my childhood is how often I meet other people who have had the same experience. How hearing repertoire played by an older brother, sister, or peers fueled their desire to learn to sing or play a musical instrument. Listening has a pull on students, enticing them with the delights of musical discovery. It encourages trying something new, unfamiliar, uncharted yet intriguing all at the same time.

Hearing another student perform a piece at a concert, church, festival, school talent show, or in the teacher's studio can provoke enthusiastic feelings in terms of their curiosity for musical exploration. That's why after every student concert, I always ask my students to identify which piece they might want to learn in the future. I pique their listening experience by playing an excerpt and suggest they listen to a recording from time to time. Especially for elementary and junior students, I repeatedly highlight pieces like Bach's *Gigue in B flat major* with its impressive, crossed hands position, Beethoven's *Fur Elise,* Mozart's *K. 331 Ronda alla Turca*, and Chopin's *Minute Waltz* as pieces that students can instantly recognize and identify. If students don't have the opportunity to hear performances of these pieces, I introduce them during their lessons, often helping students learn to play the first few bars. In this way, their experience of listening to repertoire beyond their current level serves as the effective incentive for their future explorations.

Teaching Tip

√ Listen for inspiration.

1. Listening for inspiration has many formal and informal sources.

LISTENING 003: SHARE

From MBT's Studio

At my monthly group class for junior high and high school students, I ask them to share with fellow class participants the opening phrases from a selection of their own choice. During a recent class, fourteen-year-old Jayda presented a selection she performed in the annual Students' Own Choice Concert: "Mia and Sebastian's Theme" from the movie *La La Land*. Jayda brought a recording of her selection on her phone so the other students could hear it. She also brought a printout of the first two phrases cut into one-bar segments. Jayda mixed up the order of the bars (as in shuffling a deck of cards) and asked each of the other students to pick one or two of the printed bars. After listening to the recording, students, through trial and error, placed the printed bars in order—along with each student playing the melody or combination of melody and accompaniment. Then Jayda talked about the key signature and demonstrated the various chords. Students organized themselves to play the entire selection—some playing only the melody and others only the chords. In just a few minutes, everyone could play the opening of "Mia and Sebastian's Theme" before the next students continued with their own selections.

No matter how advanced or elementary their level of playing, I want to provide frequent opportunities for students to constructively share their musical skill set with others—especially with their peers. This aspect of sharing is important because it confirms that students' listening choices, musical knowledge, and performance experience are valuable social commodities. They already possess the skill set for teaching others what they know about music and sharing insider musical shortcuts is a great way to make friends.

I also appreciate how this teen activity highlights the diversity of my students' musical interests. Previous explorations have included selections from Bruno Mars, Queen, the Beatles, Coldplay, Yiruma, Taylor Swift, Brandon Heath, Pharrell Williams, *Downton Abbey,* Tchaikovsky's *Nutcracker Suite,* and more—a wide-ranging, eclectic, and varied list as unique as my students.

Teaching Tip

√ Use listening as a first step in sharing.

1. Listening is a marvelous shortcut.
2. Sharing insider musical knowledge is a valuable social commodity.

FURTHER THOUGHTS

When I was a senior in high school preparing for an upper-level piano examination, my teacher loaned me a recording of Glenn Gould performing compositions by J. S. Bach with a few words of cautionary advice. She said, "Please, no listening to this recording more than once. I don't want you to end up playing like Glenn Gould!" Years later as I look back on her recommendation, I can't help thinking how marvelous it would be to play like Glenn Gould—even if there's not much likelihood of that ever happening. Like other teachers of her generation, she worried that listening to Gould would somehow overtake my own performance, that I wouldn't be able to handle his influence. What's ironic about her advice is that I've listened to Gould's performances of Bach throughout my entire life, and not once would I ever say that listening to him has taken over my musicianship. Quite the contrary. Listening to Gould's playing has inspired me to play as well as I possibly can!

Build On and Exercise What's Already There

Listening is the need to turn what we hear into what we play.

1. Current research has emphasized the importance of listening as the prerequisite for learning to play by ear *and* learning to play by reading. In what ways do you actively support your own students' listening? What could you do differently?

2. Students listen to music intentionally, casually, and randomly. How do you currently build on and exercise students' listening experiences? What could you do differently?

Part 3

PROJECTS

Music is everywhere.

At home. At work. At play.

With friends. With family. With crowds.
Random. Deliberate. Involved. Distracting.

Old songs. Folk songs. Pop songs. New songs.
Anthems. Incantations. Rituals. Traditions.
Jingles. Movie themes. TV shows.
Sports. Recreations. Dances.
Eating. Drinking.

Where time and place take shape.
Where memories live on.

Music is there.

Chapter 12

Non-performance Music Projects

BACKGROUND

From MBT's Studio

> Fourteen-year-old Ben informs me that he's started using musical analogies as his preferred method for explaining complex matters at school. Not a typical teenage observation you might think. However, for me it was something completely in sync with his state of mind. Particularly because Ben has been investigating his own everyday musical connections by using a project-based learning approach for the previous six months.

What do I mean by everyday musical connections? And what is project-based learning? To answer these questions, it's probably best if I do a bit of backtracking to explain how three elements came together and unexpectedly shed light on a completely new direction for my teaching.

1. *Everyday Musical Connections:* I've always been impressed by the multifaceted and unique relation that people have with music, regardless of age, socioeconomic standing, geographic context, or education. As renowned pianist Daniel Barenboim proposed, "The power of music lies in its ability to speak to all aspects of the human being. Music teaches us, in short that everything is connected."[1] At times, music may be a companion, a diversion, an interruption, a refuge, a catalyst, and a reminder. When it comes to musical connections, diversity is the characteristic of the day. Our connections with music come in all sizes and shapes, from the emotional to the intellectual, the physical to the spiritual, the individual to the collective. Of course, learning to sing or play a musical instrument can contribute in meaningful ways

to an individual's relation with music. That's where vocal and instrumental instructors come in. Yet when we consider the space music occupies in our lives, a breadth and depth of everyday musical experiences come to mind. Experiences that don't involve performance capacities, like the way a favorite tune randomly pops into your head, how elevator music sticks with you for the rest of the day, the creation and sharing of musical playlists, how you respond when music intensifies cinematic drama, how music carries meaning in TV and radio advertisements, music in religious, sports, and recreational contexts, not to mention how listening to music can span everything from intense personal involvement to complete distraction. In other words, we all have a plethora of non-performance everyday musical connections that greatly outnumber our performance-based explorations.

Teaching Tip

√ Find out about students' everyday relationship with music.

1. What is the student's musical story?
2. What do students' musical interests look like?

2. *Allsup's Disconnection:* Randall Allsup is a music educator who has written prolifically about the challenges facing contemporary music instructors. His vision of music education aims to be open, changing, and adventurous at heart. When I came upon his observation of "the disconnection between the music studied at school and the hidden or private musical world of our students,"[2] something about this quote really resonated with me. Indeed, was my teaching approach adequate in responding to my students' "hidden or private musical world?" Or was there a disconnect as Allsup suggested? Most assuredly, I recognized my attention to students' autonomy in their ongoing own choice selections was important. But was that enough? What about the plethora of non-performance everyday musical connections that occupy students' lives? What could I do to help students connect meaningfully with their private musical world, their own relation with music, their own personal character?

3. *Project-Based Learning*: Following the completion of my PhD at the University of Calgary, my supervisor encouraged me to join the Bachelor of Education faculty where project-based learning (PBL) features as a key component of the department's educational philosophy. BEd students (future teachers) explore PBL as it applies to curriculum delivery across the entire

spectrum of subjects: science, literacy, mathematics, history, sports, the arts. Immersed in this setting, it soon became clear that PBL was just what I was looking for—a solution for connecting more purposefully with my students' "hidden musical world." This approach would provide the structure I needed for students to meaningfully investigate their own everyday musical connections. I'd found a new direction for my teaching.

PROJECT-BASED LEARNING

With an emphasis on students' involvement in active and inquiry-based learning, the roots of PBL can be traced to the educational philosophies of John Dewey (1859–1952), Maria Montessori (1870–1952), and Jean Piaget (1896–1980). From a historical perspective, PBL represents a departure from Western educational systems in which teachers were primarily tasked with directing or transmitting knowledge to students. The overriding consideration in a PBL approach is that teaching is not about telling students what to learn or what to do, but about organizing experiences that prompt students to actively participate in their own learning experiences. William Kilpatrick (1871–1965), a professor at Columbia Teachers College in New York City, was instrumental in promoting PBL in the early twentieth century. He believed in learning environments that cultivate purposeful activity and student engagement. As he described in the 1918 *Teachers College Record*, "Learning of all kinds and in all its desirable ramifications best proceeds in proportion as wholeheartedness of purpose is present."[3]

PBL is a student-centered pedagogy that advances learning through genuine exploration of real-life situations, ideas, concepts, and challenges. Because PBL purposefully integrates knowing and doing,[4] students deepen their understanding of a particular subject and learn to apply what they already know in order to come up with solutions and produce results that matter. They experience, firsthand, the difference between acquiring information and putting it to use. Advocates of PBL promote numerous beneficial layers to its implementation in educational contexts including increased student engagement, opportunities for both practical and creative application, in addition to improvements in communication, interpersonal skills, critical thinking, and self-management.

To achieve results and ensure quality learning, PBL follows an intentional process in which the following four elements—student engagement, sustained inquiry, public presentations, and reflective evaluations—are integral.

Student Engagement: PBL starts by teachers acknowledging students' voice and choice in identifying a topic or question that's meaningful and doable for themselves.[5] This means students perceive the project as something that matters to them and something they want to do well. There's a feeling of authenticity[6] in the way students' choice of topic fits with their interests, culture, identity, or concerns. From another perspective, doable projects refer to scope or intent, making sure to challenge students without overwhelming them. By valuing students' reasons for learning, PBL fosters a sense of ownership in students that contrasts remarkably with passively doing an exercise or blindly following the teacher's set of directions.

Sustained Inquiry: PBL students conduct investigations that draw information from multiple sources and teachers act as instructional guides who coach them through the process. The key to sustained inquiry is that such processes take time,[7] incorporate ongoing cycles of fine-tuning, and involve equal attention to content and personal development. Teachers help students with brainstorming, with creating a framework to organize their thoughts, and with asking deeper questions. Students, through their own hands-on experience, witness how ideas emerge and evolve to subsequently fuel further questioning or investigation. Knowing that inquiry-based processes can range from nonlinear to structured and predictable to random, effective PBL teachers are attentive to the practice and thinking time necessary for students to put together their best work.

Public Presentations: At the end of a PBL investigation, students prepare a recognizable public product. Presenting results in a public setting encourages students to adopt a level of accountability that goes beyond the private exchange between an individual student and teacher.[8] This social dimension of PBL reinforces the notion of a learning community wherein students' learning is tangible and rich with potential to stimulate further discussion. An important aspect of presenting is for students to demonstrate what they know about a topic.[9] Being open to public scrutiny and input, students demonstrate how their work has value for themselves, their peers, their teachers, their parents, and their communities at large.

Reflective Evaluation: Although projects may seem to end with a public presentation, the PBL process is not complete without a final reflective evaluation. After project activities have been concluded, students and teachers intentionally debrief the project. Taking time to reflect on the content knowledge and understanding gained from the project helps students solidify what they've learned and consider how their learning might be applied elsewhere. Reflections on skills utilized may shed light on the skills students automatically bring with them and which skills may require further growth. Reflections on the project's design and implementation help students in deciding how they'll approach their next project.[10]

Your Thoughts

Project-based learning combines student engagement, sustained inquiry, public presentations, and reflective evaluation.

1. Which of the above factors are already evident in your approach as a performance teacher?
2. Which of the above factors may seem unfamiliar?

Project-based learning goes beyond teachers simply finding projects for students to complete.[11] Its framework of student engagement, sustained inquiry, public presentation, and reflective evaluation calls for the dynamic integration of knowing and doing. Furthermore, PBL rejects the portrayal of students as vessels to be filled with knowledge, instead choosing to promote and draw from their own passion, creativity, accountability, empathy, and resiliency in order to accomplish learning. The advantages of such an approach are that PBL offers teachers the structure to help students explore a wide range of topics; and PBL makes it possible for teachers to get out of students' way, empowering them to take the lead and propel investigations that teachers might never imagine.

TEACHER'S ROLE

Over the past several centuries, the master/apprentice model of instruction has dominated vocal and instrumental performance teaching in music studios, bands, orchestras, and choirs. Within this model, teachers are cast as the authoritative fount of knowledge and the primary source of feedback.[12] Music instructors maintain a top-down hierarchy for instructing students wherein carefully sequenced, linear, incremental, and standardized processes are prioritized. Often, music is presented as an autonomous art form that calls for explicit aesthetic, technical, and interpretive explorations. While the master/apprentice model remains a practical option for many music educators, there is considerable debate about the appropriateness of the current degree of reliance on the master/apprentice model in music instruction.[13]

In contrast to the master/apprentice instructional approach, the teacher's role in PBL is commonly described in terms of moving away from the "sage on the stage" to the "guide on the side."[14] PBL teachers take on the role of facilitator, that is, someone who helps to bring about an outcome by providing indirect assistance. They excel in watching, listening, asking or answering questions, challenging, offering suggestions, or lending a hand because their aim is to engage students meaningfully in the application, exploration, and extension of what they know.[15] All these points are prominently represented in education literature as affirmed by Maria Montessori: "The teacher's task is not to talk, but to prepare and arrange a series of motives for cultural activity in a special environment made for the child."[16]

Teaching Tip

√ Facilitate, collaborate, mentor, and guide students' non-performance explorations.

1. Assist with brainstorming and project development.
2. Expand and refine students' capacity for learning.

My own PBL teaching takes on a blending of diverse roles including facilitator, collaborator, provoker, mentor, guide, and resource. The diversity in this lengthy list is intentional because it's my responsibility to cultivate, support, and nurture my students as they are. While equally significant, I also have an unspoken obligation to introduce processes that expand and refine my students' capacity for learning. This means when students struggle to get started, I help them by pulling out the prominent concepts from their description to assist with organization. Elsewhere, when students become overly reliant on certain tools like visual images in their presentations, I collaborate with resources that encourage comfortable connections with written text. The underlying belief of PBL teaching is that students explore relevant experiences and that a key aspect of teaching is well-timed informative assistance. PBL instructors substantiate their teaching with philosophical values and educational principles that champion openness, awareness, and communication as vital to meaningful interactions between teachers and students.

Your Thoughts

Everyday musical connection projects require music teachers to step out of their usual performance-based instructional context.

1. What makes you nervous about everyday musical connection projects?
2. What makes you excited about everyday musical connection projects?

NOTES

1. Daniel Barenboim, *Everything Is Connected* (London: Weidenfeld & Nicolson, 2008), 134.
2. Randall Allsup, "Mutual Learning and Democratic Action Instrumental Music Education," *Journal of Research in Music Education*, 51 no. 1 (2002): 25.
3. William H. Kilpatrick, "The Project Method," *Teachers College Record*, 19 no. 4 (1918): 334.
4. Thom Markham, "Project Based Learning: A Bridge Just Far Enough," *Teacher Librarian* 39 no. 2, Canadian Business & Current Affairs Database (December 2011): 38.
5. Markham, "Project Based Learning," 39.
6. Dannon G. Cox and Karen S. Meaney, "Lights, Camera, Project-based Learning!" *Strategies* 31 no. 1 (2018): 25.
7. John Larmer, John Mergendoller, and Suzie Boss, "Gold Standard PBL: Essential Project Design Elements," *Buck Institute for Education* (2015): 2.
8. Larmer, Mergendoller, Boss, "Gold Standard," 4.
9. Acacia M. Warren, *Project-based Learning Across the Disciplines* (Thousand Oaks, CA: Corwin, 2016), 152.
10. Larmer, Mergendoller, and Boss, "Gold Standard," 3.
11. John Larmer and John R. Mergendoller, "Seven Essentials for Project-based Learning," *Educational Leadership*, 68 no. 2 (September 2010): 34–37.
12. P. Luff and D. Lebler, "Striking a Balance in Brass Pedagogy," in *Collaborative Learning in Higher Education*, edited by H. Gaunt and H. Westerlund (Surrey, UK: Ashgate Publishing, 2018), 173–77.
13. See Randall Allsup, *Remixing the Classroom* (Bloomington: Indiana University Press, 2016); R. Daniel and K. Parkes, "Assessment and Critical Feedback in the Master-Apprentice Relationship," in *Assessment in Music Education*, edited by D. Lebler, G. Carey, and S. Harrison (Springer, 2015), 107–12; H. Gaunt, "One-to-one Tuition in a Conservatoire: The Perceptions of Instrumental and Vocal Students," *Psychology of Music* 38 no. 2 (2010): 178–208; L. Latukefu and L. Verenikina, "Expanding the Master-Apprentice Model," in *Collaborative Learning in Higher Education*, edited by H. Gaunt and H. Westerlund (Surrey, UK: Ashgate Publishing, 2018), 101–9; William Westney, *The Perfect Wrong Note* (Pompton Plains, NJ: Amadeus Press, 2003).
14. Markham, "Project Based Learning," 38.
15. Steven Wolk, "Project-based Learning: Pursuits with a Purpose," *Educational Leadership*, 52 no. 3 (1994): 42–45.
16. Maria Montessori, *The Absorbent Mind* (New York: Henry Holt, 1995), 7.

Chapter 13

Giving Voice to Students

STUDENTS' EVERYDAY MUSICAL CONNECTIONS PROJECTS

During my first season of everyday musical connections (EMC) projects, I asked individual students eleven years of age and older to come up with topics they'd like to explore from their own EMC.[1] I organized a schedule of public presentations to take place every four to six weeks. As expected, students all had their own unique interests and processes.

Meaghan: At eleven years of age, Meaghan was the youngest student to take on an investigation. For her first project, she decided to explore two of her favorite songs from the movie *La La Land*. As Meaghan was unsure how to proceed, I asked her to tell me in a couple of sentences about the two songs. Then I explained how the characteristics she'd just identified could serve as an outline for her investigation. She prepared a PowerPoint presentation that included information about the movie, sound bites of its songs, and her explanation of its characteristics. After four weeks of preparation, Meaghan presented her project. At her next lesson, Meaghan and I used reflective evaluation to identify her strengths (knowledge of music and speaking skills) and weaknesses (clarity of ideas, language, PowerPoint design). Six weeks later, she presented the revised project, which included additional relevant information, in a public setting. In her final, reflective evaluation, she wrote, "There's more to a presentation than making a few slides. You need to think."

Colin: Fourteen-year-old Colin titled one of his investigations "The Benefits of Learning to Play the Piano in the Workplace." He focused on three different aspects: biological, intellectual, and enjoyment. Colin created a PowerPoint presentation with images and text. I encouraged him to make sure he included relevant musical examples. During his post-presentation reflective evaluation, Colin noted how he wanted to include a better "hook" at the beginning that would engage his audience. I suggested he needed a more deliberate summary of his presentation at the end. At his next presentation six weeks later, Colin demonstrated something quite remarkable. He spontaneously referenced two other students' presentations during his own. Following his presentation, he asked for and responded to questions from the audience. In his final reflective evaluation, Colin noted his ability to be able to think on the spot as one of the skills he used in his presentation.

Natalie: For one of her investigations, twelve-year-old Natalie chose to examine "What Makes a Good Song Good?" She interviewed several of her friends in order to come up with three elements that contribute to a good song. For each element, she selected three songs that demonstrated the element. She created a PowerPoint with text, her own transcriptions of appropriate sections, and sound-bites embedded in the slides. During her post-presentation reflective evaluation, she acknowledged that she spoke too quickly and softly to be clearly understood. I suggested she needed to practice speaking at home, streamline her language, and take more time to explain the data on each of her slides. At a second presentation four weeks later, it was obvious that her home practice and additional material brought huge improvements to her presentation. In her final reflective evaluation she wrote, "I learned that I know more about music than I thought."

Spencer: After several indecisive weeks, fourteen-year-old Spencer decided to cram until 2:00 a.m. the night before the presentation deadline in order to put together a video "mockumentary" titled *The Voice: Piano Edition*. Modeled after the TV program, Spencer filmed himself playing the roles of judge and performer. His video captured many of the TV show's signature moments and demonstrated his capacity as an entertainer and visionary producer. In his reflective evaluation, he listed creativity, editing, work effort, good mood, and time management as the skills he used. I thought it interesting that he interpreted time management as finishing his video before the presentation deadline.

During students' lessons, the amount of time devoted to these projects relates directly to their individual interests and processes. For students with large amounts of repertoire, I typically spend no more than five minutes in tweaking and clarifying their current project. Students doing upper-level Royal Conservatory of Music exams most likely don't have adequate space for taking on EMC projects. For students who are more committed to their EMC investigations than repertoire study, it seems appropriate to spend the bulk of our time in supportive discussion.

Students present their projects in multiple settings. Informally, they present to their peers during monthly group classes. Formally, students present their projects at concerts for students, parents, and guests. I divide the concert in two sections: the first half being devoted to repertoire performance and the second half to project presentations. I provide a projector with external speakers for students to connect to their laptops. I encourage presenters to ask the audience for questions at the end of their presentations. It's amazing to see audience members blown away by the insight and sophistication of students' presentations.

Your Thoughts

All students have their own unique interests and processes.

1. Which of the above projects sounds like something of interest to one of your students?
2. What do you anticipate learning about your students EMC projects?

JUNIOR HIGH THRESHOLD

When I look back on the decades of my teaching prior to initiating EMC projects, there's a particular observation that comes to mind. Namely, that as my students moved through junior high school, they frequently seemed to reach a threshold in their music studies. After years of consistent progress throughout elementary school, students were satisfied with their music studies and wanted to continue, yet stepping up the ladder to more difficult repertoire didn't really seem to attract them. Many students were content with working on a single piece of repertoire or one of their own choice over very long periods of time. Quite often, the lack of progress in learning and advancing through new material led to students quitting lessons all together. It seemed like an anticlimactic way for music studies to come to an end.

Teaching Tip

√ Generate fresh energy with personalized non-performance EMC projects.

1. Tailor explorations to students' sense of self.
2. Work within students' self-acknowledged level of achievement.
3. Use project themes to inform future directions.

What I've found remarkable is how EMC projects bring fresh energy to the threshold I observed in junior high students. Rather than getting stuck in a continuous downward spiral of diminishing practice, EMC projects confirm music as an important part of students' lives, as well as providing clues to meaningful directions for students' future repertoire and own choice explorations. Both students and I have a better sense of what might engage their evolving musical interests. In this context, students continue music lessons with a newfound enthusiasm for musical explorations that match their own sense of self and the satisfaction they have with their own level of achievement.

AMPLIFYING STUDENT'S MUSICAL PERSONA

When we consider Allsup's observation of "disconnection" and the potential for genuine interplay between music studied and students' private musical worlds, it seems certain that teachers play a major role in setting up instructional frameworks that fuel students' musical development. Looking back at my lengthy teaching career, what seems apparent is my own past tendency to address the "disconnection" by focusing exclusively on performance-based initiatives. For example, at different times and with varying intensities, I've encouraged my preteen/teen students to make and play their own compositions, develop creativity and improvisation skills, participate in structured exams and competitions as well as chamber ensemble performances, and take on increasingly challenging repertoire. While the merits of these performance-based strategies may explain why I continue to employ them in my teaching, I readily acknowledge that performance-based explorations represent only part of students' private musical worlds. There is much more to students' musical persona than performance-based initiatives.

Teaching Tip

√ Amplify students' musical persona.

1. Acknowledge students' relationship with music.
2. Let students demonstrate their disciplinary knowledge of music.
3. Listen for the social/cultural stories embedded in students' projects.

What makes it meaningful for students to tap into their own EMC? My impression is that EMC explorations achieve an outstanding accomplishment—they amplify students' musical persona. EMC projects provide the safe and trusting context for students to exercise their own dynamics of personal expression and social awareness.

In terms of personal expression, EMC projects let students know that their relations with music aren't random or insignificant. Such projects are integral to their character and personal identity. Acknowledging students' EMC is like giving their sense of self a pat on the back. Also, EMC projects provide students with the opportunity to demonstrate their own disciplinary knowledge of music, to express their emerging competency and expertise in aspects of music that are important to them, and actively implement what they know about music. Thinking about music is important because students value their efforts in making-meaning. By attempting to understand or make sense of music, students exercise their intellectual capacities. The point is that students transfer their learning from the formal lesson environment into real-life musical applications.

From MBT's Studio

> As Lorrie progressed through junior high and high school, her EMC presentations gradually evolved in sophistication and social relevancy. In an exemplary presentation, Lorrie explored the music of Billie Eilish, using the opportunity to shed light on how and why this artist's music resonates with teens such as herself; how Eilish intentionally takes on problems facing youth and gives them a voice. In another presentation, she showcased a Korean artist who sang about Instagram as a social escape platform. Lorrie pointed out shortcomings in his interpretation, in particular how Instagram may actually reduce social isolation and help people to feel more part of a community.

In terms of social awareness, through their EMC projects students demonstrate their understanding of what's going on in the world around them. Students' EMC projects carry the social/cultural stories and ideas of this generation. When students tell their musical stories, they illustrate how their narratives intertwine with and differentiate from the narratives of past generations. Students confirm their positions as thinking individuals influenced by their social context. Similar to generations before them, they make meaning of the world with what they've got. Giving voice to students' EMCs is important because such opportunities offer insight into another person's viewpoints, consciousness, and subjectivities. Given the universality of music in people's lives the world over, sharing EMCs offer a way to achieve a better understanding of one another. Over the months and years of working with students on different EMC projects, I've witnessed how this process results in an intensifying of students' musical esprit—their musical creativity, musical imagination, musical character, and musical well-being. By highlighting, interrogating, and challenging students' EMCs, I've seen how a heightened confirmation or valuing of students takes place, as well as a sense of freshness and flourishing in students' musical confidence as knowledgeable musicians. It's what impressed me in the following example:

From MBT's Studio

Following teenage Eric's first public presentation, I asked him for his impressions on how it turned out. He replied, "It's interesting how my parents have always known more than I do about everything. Last week, I think they actually saw me for the first time as being the expert. I'm the one in our family who knows the most about music!"

I couldn't help thinking about the significance of this moment in Eric's journey of growing up. Here, he saw himself as someone whose expertise could rival that of his parents—an observation that any teenager would recognize as a major moment of personal achievement.

This exploration began when three elements—everyday musical connections, Allsup's disconnection, and project-based learning—unexpectedly coalesced to shed light on a new instructional direction. What I most value is the way EMC projects accomplish much more than simply bringing together music lessons and students' private musical worlds. By giving life to students' everyday connections with music, EMC projects stand out as amazing opportunities that fuel, challenge, and champion students' understanding of who they are, how they learn, and what they know of the world around them.

FAQs

Q: Where can teachers actually see real examples of students' EMC projects? What do they look like?

A: EMC projects are available for viewing at merlinthompson.com.

Q: I'd like to try EMC projects with my teenage students but I'm not sure where or how to start. Can you provide some guidance?

A: To assist teachers with starting EMC projects, I have prepared various templates (see Appendix C). I start this journey by having students begin with "Tell Your Musical Story." Although we've most likely had many conversations regarding their musical interests, I like the way this activity broadens the discussion. It also gives me a sense of where they might possibly head with their EMC project.

To guide students in choosing an information topic for exploration, I encourage them to take on projects that are manageable in the context of weekly music lessons. Many times, they want to take on projects that are too big. For example, the history of jazz music or hip-hop music are both too large for students to manage. However, interest in jazz or hip-hop may signal that students might be interested in exploring two artists or comparing two compositions. So I guide them to take on something that's meaningful and manageable.

I use the Project Tools template to quickly guide our weekly discussions during lessons. I typically ask a few questions based on the various tools, making sure that students keep their interest within the topic of EMCs. I encourage students to create mind maps for keeping track of their ideas as they develop. Many students will want to jump in and start making PowerPoint slides much sooner than is practical.

The week before presentations, I use the Presentation Checklist to get a sense of students' progress. In this way, they have an idea of what their presentations should look like. The week after presentations, I use the EMC Project Evaluation template to share my feedback with them.

I use two settings for students' presentations. First, monthly group class for teens serve as an informal and enlightening opportunity for students to get peer feedback. In this setting, students present from their laptops. Second, on a more formal level, I have students make presentations during the final portion of my twice-yearly public concerts. In this setting, I bring a projector and external speakers that students plug into their laptops.

The Follow-up Questionnaire allows students to reflect on their presentations. Question #4 is intended to give students the opportunity to continue with their current topic or switch to another. On occasion, students may feel they didn't get as far as they'd like with a particular topic and would like to spend another period in exploration. On other occasions, students may recognize they've taken their topic as far as they're interested and would like to switch to another.

Finally, I must say that things don't always go according to my plans. Some of the best student presentations were created in the rushing few hours before the deadline with no teacher input whatsoever!

Build On and Exercise What's Already There

Exploring students' EMCs through a project-based learning approach is an amazing way to build on and exercise students' personal expression and social awareness.

1. How do you feel about connecting with students' private musical world, their own relation with music, and their own personal character?

2. In your own studio, take a look at the teenagers who might have arrived at a threshold. Which students do you think would benefit from EMC projects?

3. What's your takeaway from these chapters?

NOTE

1. Examples of students' EMC projects come from my own studio of preteens and teenagers. College and adult students may also have worthwhile projects to explore.

Part 4

CHARACTER

Music making begins with our crucible
    of personal experiences,
        a mashup of hopes and dreams,
    mastery and growth,
    momentum and contemplation.

For today's musical exploration,
      a dusting of treasured joy,
        seeds of carefully gathered knowledge,
      droplets from the vial of fear,
      a trusting dose of risk.

How can we know what our crucible will produce?

Will it be an explosion,
    an escape,
        or a triumph?

Chapter 14

Imprinted from Birth

Throughout the preceding chapters in *More than Music Lessons*, the theme of character has played an underlying role as teachers build on and exercise what's already there. In part 1, teachers respect the way character informs the identities of parents and children, and their relationships with each other. In part 2, we explored practicing as something that's essential to our own lives, character, and identity. Practicing fulfills the need that individuals have to validate their sense of self. In part 3, Allsup's observation of "disconnection" sparked efforts to engage students in non-performance projects that connect meaningfully with their private musical world, relation with music, and personal character. In part 4, the exploration of character is our central task.

When someone says, "It's just not in her character to do something like that" or "He's quite the character, isn't he?" or "They've certainly got the character needed for that job," what exactly do we mean by character? What are we hoping to convey with the word "character?" Before we examine character's etymological roots and evolution, let's start with a couple of scenarios.

From MBT's Studio

For as long as I can remember, my student Jenny has started every lesson in exactly the same manner. "Dr. Thompson," she begins, "I have a question." Sometimes Jenny needs more information or clarity. Sometimes she's looking for confirmation of her own thought processes. Sometimes her questions prompt one-statement answers. Something about her character leads her to questions and discussions. She's the only student currently in my studio who seems to be permanently questioning.

Rayna is a serious seven-year-old who carefully works out the details of her own progress. When she's got time, she helps her five-year-old sister learn the notes for easy pieces. Rayna complains that her younger sister disturbs her practice with bursts of energy. She finds it perplexing that her younger sister doesn't take learning pieces very seriously.

We find the etymological roots[1] of the word "character" in the Greek *kharakter* for "engraved mark," "symbol or imprint on the soul," and "instrument for marking," where the word originally referred to the stamp or marking impressed into wax and clay. This stamp served as the signature, monogram, or trademark of an artist, artisan, or inventor, as indicative of the personality of the maker, or the distinctive individuality of the article marked. In the seventeenth century, the meaning of "character" was extended to "a defining quality, individual feature"[2] and the word came to be associated with "the sum of qualities that defines a person."[3] So, when we talk about character, we're referring to the individual's distinctive features like Jenny's interrogative nature and Rayna's seriousness. Character is what a nurse in a birthing center may observe in an infant from day one: the busy child, the quiet one. It's the irreducible essence to which a man of eighty refers when he claims he is the same person as at age ten.

It may be useful to differentiate between historical and twenty-first-century interpretations of character as "the sum of qualities that defines a person."[4] From the seventeenth century to the mid-twentieth century, character was interpreted as individuals having dominion over personal impulses and desires in order to direct their choices toward high moral standards.[5] Historically speaking, the language most associated with the term "character" was citizenship, duty, honor, and morals.[6] Character was all about putting aside the individual's sense of self in favor of mastering the cultured self. Whereas in a twenty-first-century setting, character is about recognizing and understanding who the individual is in order to build on what's already there. Talking about a person's character in the twenty-first century, we're referring to what's at the core of a person's identity, not something manufactured, inauthentic, imposed, or artificial, but qualities naturally or inherently present. The language we associate with character is more likely about self-acceptance than self-sacrifice. We include words like "serious," "easygoing," "fragile," "vulnerable," and "dysfunctional." Words that capture individuals in all their nakedness, authenticity, and immediacy without filters or the distraction of outer adornments.

I appreciate how we may think of character like a constellation of many varied stars. Fate, authenticity, intuition, sense of self, inner voice, destiny, soul, personal essence, being true to oneself, synergy, and life force are just a few that contribute to the constellation's brilliance. These terms point to the ways different cultures and traditions have their own unique way of talking about character. Working from diverse interpretations allows us to be inclusive and sensitive to other perspectives that may enhance our own understanding of character. The combination of qualities, calling, soul, personal essence, and perceptions is what makes character unique within each person. Each individual's sense of self is set apart from another's by the way certain qualities predominate over other qualities.

Imprinted from birth, character synthesizes a person's fate and primordial calling to live life in a particular way. Philosopher Charles Taylor refers to this calling as a matter of authenticity, "There is a certain way of being human that is *my* way. I am called up to live my life in this way, and not in imitation of anyone else's. But this gives new importance to being true to myself. If I am not, I miss the point of my life, I miss what being human is for *me*."[7] Psychologist James Hillman points out, "A calling may be postponed, avoided, intermittently missed. It may also possess you completely. Whatever; eventually it will out. It makes its claim. The [calling] does not go away."[8] The Romans gave the name "genius" to this calling. The Greeks referred to it as "daimon." Among people who follow shamanistic practices like Eskimos, it is called spirit, free-soul, breath-soul. In this context, character is a dimension of how we experience life and ourselves. It involves soul, not as an object of religious belief, but as an ever-present inner voice that's always with us.

Similar to the natural force of gravity, character can work with or against us. The pull of character may keep us from going where we want to go. We can use it to create cohesiveness necessary to a meaningful life, even though we may not always hear it and may lose the connection needed to nurture it. We may be pulled away from our own character by forgetfulness, distractions, and the intensities of life.

An individual's character may be such a natural part of who they are—like breathing or sleeping—that they never really give it much thought. At the same time, individuals may rely so heavily on their character that it's inconceivable to make any decision no matter how large or small without taking it into consideration. Character is what carries our habits and mannerisms, loves and hates, predilections and passions.

Your Thoughts

Character may comprise fate, authenticity, intuition, sense of self, destiny, soul, personal essence, being true to oneself, inner voice, synergy, and life force.

1. How do you feel about this interpretation of character?
2. Which of these aspects resonates with you?

3. Which students do you already have an accurate portrait of their character, sense of self, authenticity? How might you increase your knowledge of your students' character?

Students naturally come with their own individual character imprinted from birth. They have their own blending of personal essence, inner voice, life force, destiny, soul, authenticity, sense of self. Students' well-being, thought processes, and integrity are all reflections of the very core of their being. The challenge for teachers is to take the time to recognize each student's character. Doing so may bring clarity to how teachers engage students in meaningful learning experiences. This recognition sometimes occurs in brief flashes of insight linked to a particular gesture or turn of phrase used by a student. Sometimes recognizing students' character takes place gradually over months and years.

What might students' character look like? Below is my attempt to capture a selection of my students' character in poetic verse. For teachers, see if you recognize some of your own students in the following portraits.

MY GALLERY OF STUDENT PORTRAITS

Painted in the broad brush strokes of character,
    each portrait a threshold
    where idiosyncrasy and identity
    ceaselessly converge.
The first two years she never spoke.
    Holding on to silence
    like a warm coat in January
    wrapped from head to toe.
He couldn't resist looking up
    hundreds of times in marvelous appreciation.
    The sky an endless possibility
    of stories to tell and adventures calling.
The resolute thinker.
    Knotted eyebrows and twisted jaw
    grinding through internal machinations
    serious as the Magna Carta.
Eyes dart from side to side
    searching with fragile glancing
    for a safe place to land.
The juggler out of breath.
    Arms fly and fingers rush to keep afloat
    an ever moving and constantly changing
    musical constellation.

Imprinted from Birth

A penchant for the unpredictable.
    Irrepressible delight captured
    in vaulting eyebrows and grinning cheeks.
The quiet voice of vulnerability struggles to utter
    single word answers held back by
    a paralyzing inner resistance.
Determination to match the masterful Houdini
    undoing the locks and chains of
    a most intrepid and unimaginable feat.
Creativity, invention, imagination, and originality
    overshadowed by the constant battle with
    self-sabotaging doubt and despair.
The questioner.
    Upbeat interrogations by an inquiring mind.
    What does? When is? Why? Should?
    Is there? Can? How to?
Always intentionally unmatched socks.
    Subtle intrigue? Sartorial finesse?
    Blatant disregard? Carefree nonchalance?
    Smiling with both feet!
A body with no bones.
    Posture fluid as a figure eight.
    Fingers to rival overcooked noodles before sauce.
Portraits painted yet by all means not finished.
    Each canvas a continuum of beginnings and endings
    lived out in the flurry of after school music lessons.

I appreciate how the above portraits help me in connecting with the instructional philosophy behind *More than Music Lessons*; that teachers build on and exercise what's already there. Each of the above portraits, no matter how incomplete or fleeting, reveals something of who students already are, which is important because it influences how I'll assist their musical development.

Teaching Tip

√ Get to know your student's character,
sense of self, and authenticity.

1. Watch what students do.
2. Listen to what students have to say.
3. Be prepared for students to gradually evolve.

Chapter 14

CONNECTING WITH LIFE SKILLS

From MBT's Studio

Japan, February 1986

"Can you tell me why you've enrolled your daughters in music lessons?" I ask. One by one, Mrs. Nakayama articulates the various reasons. "Time management, making improvements, brain development, discipline, carry over into other subjects, responsibility," she replies. Her list seems endless until finally she adds what I'm hoping for, "Love of music." Mrs. Nakayama interpreted music lessons as an opportunity to expand her daughters' relationship with music and the skill set that would enhance their ability to navigate daily life—their life skills. She's given me a lot to think about.

Life skills are powerful factors in our lives. With life skills, we combine the knowledge of what to do with the ability of how to do it. Life skills contribute to what people achieve over their lifetime and in their daily lives. Mrs. Nakayama mentions several in the above scenario, to which we may also add empathy, planning and decision-making, persistence, risk taking, and humor, among others.

In my own teaching, I've noticed how life skills and character have a remarkable influence on each other. How, on the one hand, a person's character may naturally prompt certain life skills and avoid others. For example, a person with a tenacious character may find it easy to persevere through a difficult task yet find it challenging to show empathy to someone with less perseverance. So the life skill of perseverance becomes strengthened, whereas empathy doesn't. On the other hand, life skills may influence how and to what degree their character flourishes. For example, the skill of reflection may strengthen a person's inherent creativity whereas without it, a person's creativity may produce limited results. Through this back-and-forth relationship, character and life skills stimulate new forms of each other that add even more to their value.

Your Thoughts

Life skills play an underlying role in music studies.

1. What have you noticed about the connection between students' character and their life skills?
2. Choose two or three of your students. What life skills do you think they bring to their music studies?

3. Which life skills do you consider essential to music studies?

The topic of life skills has been explored by several individuals and organizations. Of note Stephen Covey, in his step-by-step pathway for living in *The Seven Habits of Highly Effective People*, zeroes in on habits that provide the security to adapt to change and the wisdom and power to take advantage of the opportunities that change creates.[9] From the 1990s, Linda Kavelin Popov, Dan Popov, and John Kavelin created The Virtues Project, a comprehensive undertaking of fifty character traits.[10] Since then, The Virtues Project has spread to more than one hundred countries, and has thousands of facilitators who share its virtues-based principles and practices. Using extensive research in the 2000s, Wayne Hammond developed Resiliency Initiatives. This strength-based framework of thirty-one external and internal factors aims to help youth acquire skills to cope effectively with life challenges and to become productive and responsible adults in society.[11] What's interesting about this brief sampling of approaches to life skills is the common emphasis on development of personal and interpersonal attributes.

As an asset to my own teaching, I've found Arthur Costa and Bena Kallick's guidebook, *Learning and Leading with Habits of Mind: Sixteen Essential Characteristics for Success*, an exemplary life skills model.[12] Several aspects of this resource impressed me right from my first reading. First, with a target audience of teachers and students, Costa and Kallick use language compatible with educational settings. Second, its sixteen habits may be condensed into a smaller, more manageable framework of five principal qualities: persistence, reflection, accuracy, interdependence, and humor (note the overlap with autonomy, fluency, purpose, relatedness, and reflection from part 2). Third, persistence, reflection, and accuracy form a robust cycle for educational processes in that persistence benefits from reflection, which benefits from accuracy, which in turn leads back to persistence. Fourth, the emphasis on interdependence confirms how teachers and students may work together to generate more information, establish new ideas and possible solutions. Finally, Costa and Kallick include finding humor as a reminder that there's room for playfulness in successful learning processes.

In order to be more intentional about using the language of life skills with my students, I created a set of character cards (see appendix D) that I keep scattered on the top of my piano for quick access. With Costa and Kallick's habits of mind as a starting point, I chose additional simple actions and character traits related to successful music studies like stick-with-it, challenge, and freedom. I also wanted to give a more prominent position to concepts like cooperation, musicianship, authenticity, and gratitude. Organizing my language and printing character cards has contributed to my teaching both in weekly individual lessons and my monthly group classes.

From MBT's Studio

Sixteen-year-old Emily is comfortable with following instructions. During her lesson, we focus on learning through multiple strategies like playing with and without the book, playing with scrambled lines, and writing instructions for herself in her notebook. After I set the "get organized" card in front of her, she asks, "Why are you showing me that card?" I reply, "I want to give you a visual way to remember what we talked about during your lesson. So on the days when what we talked about and what you wrote for yourself go out the window, maybe you'll still remember that black and white card with 'get organized' on it." My goal is to strengthen Emily's skill of independently taking charge in contrast to relying on my instructions.

In my monthly teen group class, we use the final ten minutes to examine the character cards. I typically ask participants to choose two or three that express where they are that day. On occasion, students pick cards that relate to their strengths, like Kevin who picks "creativity" and "imagination" cards that match perfectly with his character. Another month, Kevin picks "refine and rework" and "challenge" as an indication that he's thinking about stepping out of his usual pattern. When Jennifer picks "take a risk" and explains that even though I'm always encouraging her to use her body more when she plays, she knows she never really does. With picking "take a risk," it feels like she's stretching her vulnerability of character in a safe and meaningful way.

When I consider the relationship between character and life skills, I always keep in mind how character serves as a personal anchor for life skills. And how, without character as an anchor, the acquisition of life skills may turn insincere and inauthentic. When I suggest Emily consider expanding her skill set, I know that she'll view her journey through the lens of her own sense of self. When Kevin and Jennifer indicate they're considering something new on their musical journeys, I know that their intentions will most assuredly acknowledge their own character. I recognize that without a meaningful connection between life skills and students' own character, there's a high probability their efforts won't go very far; that they will abandon their explorations because it just doesn't feel like it connects with who they are. Knowing about my students' character, authenticity, and sense of self tells me a lot about what we might anticipate in exploring life skills that match their character and what adjustments might be necessary in taking on life skills that put their character to the test.

To facilitate music study as a vehicle for social and personal growth, I use age-sensitive strategies with students. For elementary school students, my strategy is to sow seeds that encourage and expand their awareness and mastery of their actions. I help them get comfortable with using the language of life skills and make necessary adjustments to accommodate a variety of students.

From MBT's Studio

Seven-year-old Leah is an active student with traces of ADHD. She is curious, easily distracted, at times enthusiastic, and at other times discouraged with learning. My focus during lessons is to connect her with language that describes the qualities of what she's doing. There is a constant back-and-forth between musical and character aspects. For character aspects, I choose a character card and set it in front of her on the piano after her playing. We chat briefly about what it means. Typically, it's not long before she has an entire collection of cards that might include "cooperation," "patience," "accuracy," "thinking first," and "persistence." At the end of her lesson, we choose two or three cards to record in her notebook as reminders for her home practice. As months go by, Leah gradually gets comfortable with talking about her own musical progress with the descriptive language of the character cards.

In my monthly group class for elementary school students, I include an activity called You're the Teacher. The goal is for students to demonstrate something they think the other students should know about. It's an activity that draws from the principal themes of reflection and accuracy, wherein students need to think about what they'll demonstrate, execute their demonstration with accuracy, and explain the importance of their demonstration. It's inspiring to watch, like when five-year-old Penny demonstrates hugging fingers and explains how it can strengthen any student's fingers. She's totally in charge of her reflection and accuracy.

With junior/high school students, my focus is on deepening students' awareness, reflection, and understanding of their own personal perspective and their interactions with others. I continue to use individual lessons and group classes as the fertile ground for explorations that recognize students' sense of self. (See the above teen examples of Emily, Kevin, and Jennifer.) Character cards may provide a launching pad on occasion. For this age group, I introduce yearly reflective assignments (see chapter 10) to give students the opportunity to summarize their thoughts. What's interesting is how these strategies contribute an additional layer to students' independence and ownership (see chapter 2) and students' autonomy (see chapter 6).

Teaching Tip

√ Make meaningful connections between students' life skills and their sense of self and character.

1. Use age-appropriate vocabulary.
2. Tailor instructional strategies to match students' character.

NOTES

1. As of May 1, 2021, https://www.etymonline.com/search?q=character+.
2. Ibid.
3. Ibid.
4. Ibid.
5. Warren Sussman, *Culture as History: The Transformation of American Society* (New York: Random House, 2012).
6. James Davison Hunter, *The Death of Character: Moral Education in an Age without Good or Evil* (New York: Basic Books, 2001).
7. Charles Taylor, *The Ethics of Authenticity* (Cambridge, MA: Harvard University Press, 1991).
8. James Hillman, *The Soul's Code* (New York: Ballantine Books, 2017).
9. Stephen Covey, *The Seven Habits of Highly Effective People* (New York: Free Press, 1989).
10. L. K. Popov, D. Popov, and D. Kavelin, *The Virtues Project*. https://virtuesproject.com
11. Wayne Hammond, *Understanding the Resiliency Framework* (Resiliency Initiatives, 2003).
12. Arthur Costa and Bena Kallick, *Learning and Leading with Habits of Mind* (Alexandria, VA: ASCD, 2008).

Chapter 15

Character and Music Lessons

Learning to sing or play a musical instrument is recognized for its meaningful connection to personal development. As emphasized in the Child's Bill of Rights from the National Association for Music Education (formerly Music Educators National Conference) Clause 7, music lessons provide fertile ground for character explorations:

> As their right, all children must have the opportunity to grow in music knowledge, skills, and appreciation so as to bring joy and satisfaction to their lives, challenge their minds, stimulate their imaginations, and exalt their spirits.[1]

Following World War II and the devastation of Japan, violinist and founder of the Suzuki method, Shinichi Suzuki, added a philosophical layer to his vision of music study and performance. In 1947, Suzuki expanded the Mother-Tongue Approach in music teaching that he originally developed in the early 1930s. With children's well-being in mind, he encouraged teachers to nurture the hearts of children through music and make character development an integral element in music instruction. Suzuki's philosophy of music as a vehicle for creating a better world is fundamental to the Suzuki method and strongly supported by teachers and parents.

The National Association for Music Education (NAfME)[2] and Shinichi Suzuki[3] highlight music as a fundamental uplifting for the human spirit. Their interpretation of music as a social and personal change agent is something music teachers can readily support because of their own personal experiences with music. Namely, that listening to and performing music sparks the flame that is the individual's sense of self. No matter how much time students spend at the instrument, no matter how difficult or easy the repertoire, no matter what level students achieve, music connects meaningfully with notions of life force, soul, personal essence, authenticity, and being true to oneself.

Your Thoughts

NAfME and Suzuki method teachers make strong statements about music's potential for uplifting the human spirit.

1. How do you feel about the connection between music and the human spirit?
2. How do you incorporate this idea in your teaching?
3. What may be holding you back?

EXERCISING CHARACTER

To stimulate deep connections between students' personal thought processes and their musical performances, I developed the following poetic prose resources. My typical approach is to ask junior high and high school students to read one of the paragraphs, internalize their thoughts, and permeate their musical performance accordingly.

- Music performance is perfect for exercising patience. Try performing with the patience of a mountain that's been here since the beginning of time. An immoveable solemnity of stone on stone. Or think of patience as the encouragement of warming sun on snow, whose tender rays set in motion a spring rivulet of trickling twists and turns.
- A pianist's fingertips must be generous, knowing, and curious. Just as the seamstress's nimble touch grasps the fabric to understand its character, story, and destiny, the pianist's fingertips must release the meaning behind eighty-eight black and white keys. How else to evoke the brilliance of a new day, to send messages of hope and promise, to transform feelings, memories, and images into sound?
- "Being a musician is to see the world in song," words of amazing sharpness spoken by a savvy teenager. A resounding observation that sweeps with the sudden upshot of a kite freshly caught by a summer's breeze. Imagine the dawning delight, first in mystification and then with rapture at listening with our eyes and seeing with our ears. Could musical discovery be any more thrilling?

- Faith has an immeasurable, enduring influence on what musicians may accomplish. So have faith in yourself. Like water freshly drawn from the darkness of a well and lifted out into the light, play with the clarity of knowing who you are. But that's not all. Also have faith in others near and far. Grip firmly the hands of those you trust. Let them pull you—better yet—catapult you into the uncharted.
- When musicians play with gratitude in their performances, they humbly affirm the visible and invisible beams of goodness in their lives. The shafts of dignity and empathy that come from being cared for by others, by nature, or by a higher power. The double-edged beauty of trust and its partner—risk. The honor of unconditional support and respect. The enormous boost in being accepted by others and accepting of yourself. Practicing gratitude decreases isolation and increases optimism. It regulates self-indulgence and magnifies community. It's something we can do any time or place. Not to mention it's 100 percent free! So go ahead. What are you grateful for?
- To play for God is to engage in conversation with an invisible, transcendent, and infinitely unknowable source. God speaks in everything that is and resonates in the depths of our own soul, yet most remarkably has no voice. Through music, our versatile conversational tool, the duality of sharp questions and meaningful answers plays out. *How shall I live my life? Why is there darkness and shadow?* Such interrogations have their place. Likewise, so do soulful understandings. *Follow paths of wisdom and wonder. Do what needs to be done.* From music's opening upbeat until the final cadence fades away, prayerful conversations reveal a wholeness of mystery, gratitude, and hope. Play for God.
- Courage is a curious blending of genuineness and vulnerability. For music students, vulnerability can easily inhibit their confidence in learning repertoire, acquiring skills, and performing for others. Being courageous means opening our soul to who we are. Like the blindfolded tightrope walker who takes the first slippery step in a tumultuous rainstorm, knowing the only way to get to the windblown other side with hands tied behind back is to keep taking more slippery steps.
- Self-expression and freedom. Through musical explorations, we care for our sense of self by honoring its expression, by giving our character time and opportunity to reveal itself. Often, we may think of freedom as getting away from being controlled by something or someone else. But, there's more to freedom than that. There's what we may do in the open space of freedom. The opportunity to cultivate more of the person we already are. For our sense of self to flourish with honesty and without hesitation.

Chapter 15

EMPATHY STARTERS

Empathy is frequently defined in terms of walking in another person's shoes, a description that shortchanges how curiosity, imagination, and connection may contribute to empathetic processes. How might music students develop empathy in their performances? Try the following exercise and see how curiosity, imagination, and connection provide mortar for students' empathetic musical interpretations. With students in late elementary school, I typically ask them to choose between two or three lines as a catalyst for performance:

Take an angry building for a stroll.
Wear the shadow of a great tree as a cloak.
Soar alongside a falcon.
Console a street signal's frustrations.

Wipe away the moon's tears.
Get directions from a sunbeam.
Make friends with the color red.
Take a trip to the furthest star.

Stroke the backbone of a mountain range.
Visit the museum of unnamable objects and touch everything.
Give gravity a lesson in sharing.
Make an emotional slurpy and drink it.

Dance the thunderstorm ballet.
Shop in an insanely chaotic store.
Respond to a willow's complaints.
Ask a dog hard questions.

Shake hands with the color blue.
Collect objects with magical qualities and use them.
Choose nicknames for grains of sand.
Soothe the sore spots in a sidewalk.

Release a parachute of dandelion tufts.
Grow wishes in both hands.
Implore a window to reveal its story.
Tell yellow how to make friends.

Get flying tips from a hummingbird.
Do the opposite of diving.
Gather garlands of gratitude.

TALKING ABOUT SOUL

I created the following explorations for junior high and high school students. My aim is to build on the various interpretations that my students may bring to the idea of soul:

- Soul in five descriptive phrases. The invisible depth that penetrates every breath, every blink, every thump of my beating heart. The dependable companion hidden among motionless memories in an unknown place. The disciplined guardian, though not a guard, who holds but cannot restrain the agony of shattered dreams. The lightning bolt startling in its stunning revelation somewhere on an interior horizon. The fullness that flourishes in peals of unrestrained laughter and sings choruses of asymmetrical songs. Play with soul.
- Music makes an excellent playground for exercising the soul. Take self-forgiveness for example. To forgive yourself means exercising goodwill in the face of failures or regrets. Musical playgrounds abound with an endless array of distressing occurrences. Wrong notes. Excessive physical tensions. Anxiety. Unpleasant tones. Memory blanks. Procrastination. Runaway and rigid tempi. Fatigue. Distresses we often associate with losing control. However, there's a difference between striving for and being obsessed with excellence, between achieving flexibility and giving into haphazardness, between attending to soulful needs and enforcing intellectual ends. Self-forgiveness shifts away from perfectionist shame and guilt to wrap the soul in authentic feelings of acceptance and care.
- Another musical exercise for the soul: joy. When fingers take flight and lips set to buzzing, when throats magnify vibrations and feet tackle the beat, when musical swellings drench performers in unprepared pitches, when cascading glissandos meet congregating notes, when melodies sweep with jubilation, when nonsensical meanderings modulate, when minor befuddles major, when chords rise in union, when jagged rhythms clear the homeward track and tempi quicken a slagging stride, it's joy in all its musical extravagance and innocence, extremities and simplicities that enlivens my soul. Now, one more time, from the beginning with joy. When fingers . . .

Chapter 15

CHARACTER REFLECTIONS

These final offerings were created for junior high and high school students with the aim of stimulating conversation and empowering students' performance:

- Reflective space may be hard to achieve in a world where global connection is just a click away. Musicians need space to think for themselves outside the tunnel of virtual reality and convenience of social networking. Kudos to those who routinely disconnect from the noisy insistence of modern technology. By limiting sensory input, musicians make the most of what reflection has to offer—a sure means to curtailing sensory overload. It's a case where sensory deprivation may actually heighten sensory flourishing.
- Embrace the shadow. It's no secret that we live with competing internal qualities. Right and wrong. Ideal and reality. We favor confidence over fear. Strength over weakness. We champion good over bad. Perfect over flawed. Light over shadow. Yet prioritizing positive traits and minimizing negative attributes may mean we inadvertently bypass the wholeness of who we are. It's like building a highway that runs past amazing vistas without ever coming in contact with the garbage dump. The key to embracing the shadow is taking ownership and responsibility for the entire spectrum of our internal qualities. To be honest with ourselves and have the courage to integrate calm and chaos, understanding and anger, success and adversity. To make pathways for both light and shadow.
- Persistence. The long, circuitous road that stretches across horizons vast as the prairies, that loops and zigzags with the finesse of a rogue hockey player, that sweeps with the smoothness of a summer's lake at sunset, that doubles back on itself without warning, that feels the pang of frustration's unsolicited companionship, that relaxes in the calm cool breeze of a temporary oasis, that rejoices in the sun's rejuvenating rays, that confounds with a propensity for dead-ends and blind turns, that knows all too well the markers of time in minutes, hours, days, weeks, and months to the finish line. Persistence.
- Around and through us swirls the dirty grit of injustice. Shadows of impenetrable darkness cling to us as if we have no will of our own. Caught breathless, paralyzed, and blinded by the inequality of humankind, we step back in self-protection, giving way to our own brokenness. Yet, if we allow, if we persist, if we listen, we may weave together deeper truths. Garlands of understanding and values left behind or difficulties unanswered for so long. Pangs of conflict trigger the bugle's reveille. A calling for the soul's presence on the dusty, dark path of healing, courage, and renewal ahead.

- Solitude. Safely stored in a corner of my soul, steadfast as the sky and precious as joyful tears, music comforts and protects solitude like well-worn gloves molded to catch the quiet grooves and deeply felt creases brought on by our incessant need to hold on. Sometimes music joins solitude to travel hand in hand, traversing oceans and continents without compass or maps to bask in the passing of time. Music intertwines with solitude to craft wordless stories woven from depths buoyed by laughter, lifted in joy, torn by conflict. Sometimes music and solitude seem far away as the gleam of a distant star on a crisp winter's evening. Sometimes so close the nuances of every phrase penetrate solitude inseparable as the sweet fragrance that permeates the rose petal's voluptuous curve.

My goal in weaving threads of students' character through music performance is for students to gain experience with expressing who they are, to facilitate explorations that build on and develop their integrity, and ensure opportunities for students to exercise more of the unique individuals they already are. Musical landscapes provide safe and stimulating spaces for students to explore all kinds of challenging questions. For example, "What are you grateful for at this moment? What does joy look like in your life? Why is vulnerability important? What action does social justice require from you?" This means engaging students in compelling conversations and listening to what they have to say about music, themselves, and life. In the process of students finding out about themselves, they also remarkably get to know who I am as a person, musician, and teacher. And as we develop deep understanding of each other, we may find more ways of seeing in each other the things we mutually care about.

Teaching Tip

√ Making music is the perfect workout for human character.

1. Play with gratitude. Be generous.
2. Blend vulnerability with genuineness.
3. Cultivate joy and self-forgiveness. Light and shadow.

Exercising my awareness of students' character and engaging their own character self-awareness helps me to enhance their musical development. A reminder that musical development may be best addressed when teachers take into consideration who their students are and students share in that ongoing process. In this way, building on students' character, personal essence, sense of self isn't an additional instructional activity. It's a fundamental thread woven into the fabric of music teaching that invites teachers and students to be observant, to engage with personal language, to participate in meaningful discussions, ask complicated questions, and pursue complex answers. The point is that exercising character awareness doesn't derail effective music teaching. It enhances the instructional process of students learning how to sing or play a musical instrument.

MORE THAN MUSIC

From MBT's Studio

September 2019
Following a decade of music lessons, I ask my student Kyle to describe his takeaway from this experience. He responds with an audio recording in which he highlights various key points. Kyle explains how through piano, he's developed a willingness to open up to himself, others, and in his social life. From his musical explorations he's learned about honesty, about what it means to experience and accept emotions from frustration to celebration. He concludes with a compelling statement about how music has helped him to develop his own voice.

Internationally renowned pianist Igor Levit defends his stance as an engaged musician in an interview with Alex Ross. Music has astonishing powers of communication, he affirms, but it cannot name things. To be free requires employing your own senses. To hear, to see, to feel, to smell. Music allows us to feel this kind of freedom. "But music is not a substitute, it cannot be a substitute. Not for truth, not for politics, not for human understanding and sympathy. It cannot be a substitute for calling racism racism. It cannot be a substitute for calling misogyny misogyny. It can never be a substitute for being a wakeful, critical, loving, living, and active citizen."[4]

Each in their own individual way, Kyle and Levit shed light on the transformative power of musical experiences. How music punctuates the highs and underscores the lows of our everyday lives. How music solidifies emotional bonds with events and people. Music has the power to excite, calm, anchor, console, agitate, distract, and drive who we are and what we do. From pop to classical to jazz, folk, and more, music has the power to exercise a person's character, sense of self, and soul in the fundamental way a breeze activates the sails of a windmill.

Kyle and Levit also take their relationships with music one step further to honor their personal and social voice, to acknowledge how music may give rise to thoughts we might never have known we are capable of. How musical experiences may release the valves of personal reflection and interpersonal awareness. However, as Levit points out, even with all its power of communication, music cannot be a substitute for our own involvement in terms of expressing our own thoughts. For calling out injustice when we see it. For standing up for the kind of world we want to live in and how we'll contribute to it. Expressing our thoughts means uttering them out loud and making them heard.

Your Thoughts

Musical explorations punctuate the highs and lows of our everyday lives.

How can you help students in exploring empathy, freedom, gratitude, or courage on their own musical journey?

Most uncanny is how this exploration of character and music ties back to the themes of part 2: autonomy, fluency, purpose, relatedness, and reflection. For example, musical explorations open spaces for individuals to experience the autonomy and fluency of who they are. Spaces that allow individuals to take direction of their own lives. We assemble our playlists of favorite selections that synchronize with our own inner voice, that display our own character. We cannot keep from expressing our sense of self in musical performances. We give what we have of ourselves to the repertoire we play. Through repeated engagement in meaningful musical experiences, we extend and expand our abilities. We bring confidence and a feeling of fluency to our own character. Who we are is naturally integrated, strengthened, and internalized through music.

No matter how directly or indirectly, grandiose or minimal, the purposes we pursue have an impact on who we are. Purpose provides the backstory for why we participate in musical activities. Whether it's performing or listening to music, purpose may involve music as distraction, engagement, protection, consolation, and motivation for our sense of self. Character goes a long way to explain our deep-seated desire to direct our own lives, to do things well, to have purpose in what we do, and to make contributions in the service of something larger than ourselves.

Although it's natural to think of character as a private and personal undertaking, there is something about who we are that recognizes our need for relatedness. Musical experiences can fulfill our need for relationships and make us feel like we're part of a community. Music reminds us that we have an attachment to the world and the people around us. It offers confirmation that our sense of self belongs to something greater than ourselves.

Finally, with music as catalyst for personal freedom and as release for our inner voice, it's important to remember that treating character with dignity demands critical reflection of our efforts and what's going on around us. Character flourishes in an environment that values others, recognizes individual talents, respects differences, provides equal opportunity, acknowledges the value of criticism, and ensures no obstacles to freedom of expression. In this context, who we are also invokes consideration of how we'll contribute to the vast world in which we participate.

Teaching Tip

√ Music may empower us to stand up for something larger than ourselves.

1. Bring forward empathy, dignity, and wonder.
2. Support students in exploring what's already there.
3. Help students expand their personal confidence through gentle explorations.

Music teachers cannot predict what bit of information, snippet of conversation, or deliberate exercise will result in significant support for students' character, sense of self, and inner voice. Yet in the weeks, months, and years of lessons, there seems to be endless opportunity for teachers to foster conditions sensitive to who students are. Teachers' curiosity, improvised thoughts, serendipitous intuitions, and rogue imaginations provide support for students' character.

The beauty with character is how it's already there. It's an affirmation of our humanity that's ready to go with sense of self, soul, personal essence, fate, life force, destiny, and inner voice. Using music to exercise students' character means teachers facilitate discussions and performance opportunities that empower students to express their own authentic voice. Through such explorations, students become more familiar with their sense of self and strengthen the picture of who they are. And, in taking musical steps forward and backward, students work through the big and small decisions that inevitably impact how they see themselves and what they're going to do with life.

FAQs

Q: I appreciate how part 4 focuses on creating conditions that support students' character. What suggestions do you have for music teachers to get the ball rolling?

A: Music teachers have a lot on their plate. And the idea of introducing another layer to their teaching may appear to be daunting. So, I want to emphasize that personal interactions in support of students' character may already be in place. What can teachers do to build on this aspect?

My most practical suggestion is to create your own set of character cards. (See appendix D.) Modify the list of words to synchronize with concepts and ideas that support your teaching. Keep the cards spread out in a location where they're visible and easily accessible. I spread my cards on top of my grand piano. Use the activities for individual students and group lessons described in this chapter. I have found that printing a wordlist doesn't work for me. I need individual cards with large fonts that are easy to read.

I also use character exercises, empathy starters, talking about soul, and character reflections with my students. For access in my studio, I have them in printed format. For online lessons, I email the documents to my students so they may access them during their lessons and practice sessions. Please feel free to copy and paste any of these materials.

Build On and Exercise What's Already There

Character: sense of self, authenticity, life force, soul, calling.

1. How do you feel about students exercising their character through musical explorations?
2. How does building on students' musical exploration of empathy, freedom, gratitude, or courage have an impact on their daily lives?

NOTES

1. As of May 1, 2021: https://nafme.org/my-classroom/journals-magazines/nafme-online-publications/childs-bill-of-rights/
2. Ibid.
3. Shinichi Suzuki, *Nurtured by Love* (Hicksville, NY: Exposition Press, 1969).
4. Alex Ross, "The Fearless Pianist," *The New Yorker*, May 18, 2020.

Chapter 16

Finale: Our Shared Humanity

At the time of writing *More than Music Lessons: A Studio Teacher's Guide to Parents, Practicing, Projects, and Character*, we find ourselves facing the unprecedented challenges of a global pandemic along with social unrest, environmental concerns, and economic instability. This extraordinary combination, at times unsettling and other times hopeful, is testing our capacity for taking action while pushing us to think about what kind of world we want to live in and how we'll contribute to it. In a world with enormous challenges, where it often seems like there's a lot going on and limited time to respond, we may well wonder what any of us can do to make a difference. What will it take to make the world a better place for all of us? How can music teachers even think of taking this on?

I respond to these unprecedented times with a call for action—an invitation for music teachers to empower their teaching with notions of humanity. I urge teachers to get to the heart of the matter, to break through barriers, to engage students in personally and socially meaningful explorations, to teach in ways that challenge students within and beyond the music studio. Our teaching is important and meaningful because capacities that support thriving music education settings also provide resilient foundations for families, neighborhoods, and institutions that bring caring individuals and communities together.

Using a framework of parents, practicing, projects, and character, I've shed light on what music teachers are positioned to accomplish. Listen. Learn. Collaborate. Reflect. These simple actions demonstrated throughout *More than Music Lessons* form the backdrop of weekly lessons for periods often stretching into years. Music teachers work with individuals and groups in face-to-face interactions that build personal expression and social awareness. We facilitate endless life-affirming and life-challenging explorations. Knowing that students move through cycles of confidence and insecurity, we give time, thought, and energy to long journeys that belong only partially to us and mostly to our students. We work in an environment resonating with opportunity to recognize, awaken, stimulate, and validate our students' inner voice, their authenticity, and their character.

How can music teachers follow through on parents, practicing, projects, and character? What's the next step? My impression is that when music teachers value others for who they are and what they do, they change the world for the better. They make important statements about diversity and inclusion. About recognizing each other and our fundamental connectedness. Our work starts with understanding, accepting, and caring for others as they are, in contrast to what we might want or think they should be. It involves our fragility and vulnerability, resilience and strength. Our potential to overcome challenges and realize dreams as individuals and communities. It's all about music teachers having awareness and being intentional about what they do. Not easily done, but no one said it would be easy.

My request in *More than Music Lessons* is sincere and direct: for music teachers to nurture their students' sense of self, relationships with others, and connection to the world around them. Beyond teaching the skills of musicianship, I encourage vocal and instrumental music teachers to listen, learn, collaborate, and reflect so that our teaching strengthens relationships between people, builds empathy, and supports character with loving respect for the individual. We might even think of making music as the vibrant synthesis of freedom, awareness, and self-expression ideally suited to build on and exercise the flourishing of our shared humanity. A worthwhile set of goals for an extraordinary era.

Teaching Tip

√ Build on and exercise the flourishing of our shared humanity.

1. Strengthen relationships.
2. Build empathy.
3. Support character.

All around us life is being lived with music. Music teachers, students, and parents all know what it's like to live with music. It's our enduring companion and welcome friend. Music is everywhere and always there. We might even find it hard to think of a time when music wasn't part of our lives. My hope is that through music we may realize a future for ourselves and generations to come that reflects the very best of humanity. That each of us, in our own unique way, may truly, and with great abundance, experience the richness that music and life have to offer. As a final gesture, I would like to share "A Music Teacher's Testament," a work of poetic verse that mirrors the spirit of *More than Music Lessons*. I offer it as an accompaniment to teachers building and exercising rigorous and joyful musical explorations in the weeks, months, and years of music teaching still to come.

A Music Teacher's Testament

by Merlin B. Thompson

I am a music teacher. Whether by intention, by accident, or by calling.
    Honored to nurture musical journeys.
    Privileged to walk alongside my students.
My days are rich with meaning and value.
    I open doors. I show the way. I jostle. I step aside.
    I treasure when students take the reins.
Smiles bind us one to another.
    Conversations expand our mutual understanding.
    Gestures tell stories of their own.
    Dreams abound in the twinkle of an eye.
Rhythms of certainty and uncertainty punctuate the path.
    Safety and security cushion the journey, while
    Risk fills the space of predictability with fresh horizons.
    Willingness sparks the flame of exploration.
Fear inflicts wounds on success and shame on failure.
    Surrender is not an option.
    Fear is my friend the whistleblower.
Music teaching resonates with energies of the universe.
    We hold it in our hands and in our imaginations.
    It fuels our love for each other.
    It anchors homes and communities.
My commitment is to serve all with grace and generosity.
    The enthusiastic. The dedicated.
    The busy. The stressed out. The troubled.
No matter the twists and turns, celebrations and setbacks,
    I play my part for music and humanity.
    I affirm the wonder of who students are.
I bring empathy, dignity, and gratitude
    to the work that needs to be done.
This is my testament.

(© Music Teachers National Association 2021)

Appendix A
Challenges

As a tool for developing fluency, challenges typically demonstrate several important characteristics. Challenges cannot be so hard that they are unachievable, nor so easy that they appear worthless. Challenges may instill inspiration and dedication one day, and not the next. Challenges may be applied to an entire piece, to certain bars within a piece, and activities outside the repertoire. They may extend over long periods of time and short-term processes. Furthermore, challenges always require age- and level-appropriate considerations for successful implementation. Please adjust the following piano student challenges to appropriate challenges for singers and instrumentalists.

CHALLENGES FOR ELEMENTARY PIANO STUDENTS

Tone Challenges

- Play with consistent legato and staccato tone.
- Experiment with flicking tone, poking tone.
- Play legato instead of staccato, staccato instead of legato.
- Experiment with intensities of energy: physical, emotional, spiritual.

Visual Challenges

- Play with eyes closed.
- Play while watching only the right or left hand.
- Play with one hand covered.

- Play while looking at the ceiling, or out the window, or a picture on the wall, etc.

Physical Challenges

- Play with grabbing fingers, especially engaging the finger pads.
- Play with flexible fingers, play with stiff fingers.
- Experiment with open and closed hand position.
- Experiment with low wrist position, high wrist position, normal wrist position.
- Play with walking fingers moving gently toward the fallboard and back to the edge of the keyboard.
- Play leaps with a horizontal circular motion.
- Play while standing up.
- Experiment with engaging the core.
- Experiment with breathing and flow.

Tempo Challenges

- Play at a relaxed tempo.
- Play at the tempo of the piece.
- Play at a slightly quicker tempo.
- Play as quickly as possible.

CHALLENGES FOR JUNIOR PIANO STUDENTS AND ABOVE

Tone Challenges

- Play with consistent tone.
- Play with melody and accompaniment tone.
- Experiment with flicking tone, bonk tone, pong tone.
- Play with dynamics: p, mp, mf, or f.
- Play with shaping the phrase: crescendo and diminuendo.
- Play with opposite dynamics and exaggerated dynamics.
- Play legato instead of staccato, staccato instead of legato.
- Play four-, two-, and one-bar phrases.
- Experiment with intensities of energy: physical, emotional, spiritual.

Visual Challenges

- Play with eyes closed.
- Play while watching only the right or left hand.
- Play with one hand covered.
- Play while looking at the ceiling, or out the window, or a picture on the wall, etc.

Physical Challenges

- Play with grabbing fingers, especially engaging the finger pads.
- Play with flexible fingers, play with stiff fingers.
- Experiment with low wrist position, high wrist position, normal wrist position.
- Play with walking fingers moving gently toward the fallboard and back to the edge of the keyboard.
- Playing leaps with a horizontal circular motion.
- Play while standing up.
- Experiment with breathing and flow.
- Play with breathing at the beginning of the phrase: inhale on the upbeat, exhale on the downbeat.
- Play while engaging the core.

Tempo Challenges

- Play at a relaxed tempo.
- Play at the tempo of the piece.
- Play at a slightly quicker tempo.
- Play as quickly as possible.
- Play with speeding up, slowing down.
- Play with pauses, physically stopping and mentally preparing for the next section or note.
- Play without pauses.

Beat Challenges

- Play with hands together and hands separately while tapping the beat with the foot.
- Play with hands together and separately while marching. This activity is valuable for duple and quadruple time signatures.

- Play with hands together and separately while swaying or swinging the upper body side to side. This activity is valuable for triple time signatures.
- Play with one hand while keeping every beat in the bar with the other hand.
- Play with one hand while keeping the subdivided beat in the bar with the other hand.
- Play with one hand while keeping one beat to the bar with the other hand.
- Clap the rhythm of a section while counting out loud.
- Play with hands together and hands separately while counting out loud.

Practicing with the Score Challenges

- Play with one hand while tracking the score with the other hand.
- Say the finger numbers out loud while playing with one hand and tracking the score with the other hand. This activity is ideal for small amounts of fingering and trills. Not practical for entire pieces.
- Say the finger numbers out loud without tracking.
- Sing the note names or solfège names while playing with one hand and tracking the score with the other hand. Especially valuable for short trills and turns.
- Sing the note names or solfège names while playing with one hand without tracking.
- Play with the score, without the score.

CREATIVITY CHALLENGES FOR ALL LEVELS

- Play with colors to inspire the tone quality: red, blue, pink, black, etc.
- Play with emotions to inspire the tone quality: happy, sad, frustrated, nervous, calm, etc.
- Play with your imagination, care.
- Play with your musicianship, artistry.
- Play with beauty—delight, curiosity, wonder.
- Play the teacher's favorite way, the composer's favorite way.
- Put "heart and soul" into your playing.
- Invite a "spirit helper" to be part of your playing.

Appendix B

Parent Letter and Teenager Letter

PARENT LETTER

August 2020

Dear Jennifer and Osborn Smith,

Thank you so much for all your support during these recent months of music lessons. Before we continue with more lessons, I want to ask you to sit down with Jasmine for a casual conversation about the piano. The point is to explore ideas both from Jasmine and you as parents. To give you some guidance, I suggest the following for your conversation.

Musical Goals: you may want to talk about things like: finishing pieces hands together and right hand melodies, having fun, learning a popular song, learn a duet with Mom or Dad, listening to the recording. Start with musical goals Jasmine has already achieved and see what other musical goals you can come up with.

Life Skills: three aspects stand out. 1. Persistence—stick-with-it, being flexible, independence, empathy, and taking risks. 2. Reflection—making sure there's critical thinking about what's working and not. 3. Accuracy—performance excellence, refinement, and precision. Start by talking about life skills already in place before discussing life skills to add on.

Family Home Life: you may want to talk about things like: playing a weekly home concert, learn a duet with Mom or Dad, prepare a selection for the family to sing, choosing favorite pieces. Start with a review of what's already working and see what you might add on.

What seems remarkable is how **Musical Goals, Life Skills,** and **Family Home Life** overlap and intertwine with each other. When you pay attention to what's happening in one area, you'll most likely see there's good reason for it to have an impact on another area. So, for example, if Jasmine sets a Musical Goal to complete two pieces hands together, it makes sense that she would be sharing her accomplishment in frequent home concerts. Or for example, if Jasmine focuses on Persistence, it will have an impact on her Accuracy of performance and help with her goal of completing pieces hands together. In this way, learning to play the piano is an excellent investment in three vital areas.

To organize the information, please make a chart to put in Jasmine's practice binder.

Musical Goals	Currently in place	To start working on
Life Skills	Currently in place	To start working on
Family Home Life	Currently In place	To start working on

See where your conversation leads and what kind of information you can put together with parent and child input. I look forward to hearing about what you discovered in your conversation with Jasmine on September 9.

Sincerely,

Merlin Thompson

Appendix B

TEENAGER LETTER

August 2020

Welcome Back Noah!

Lessons are resuming just around the corner. Please take some time to respond to the following areas for discussion during your first lesson in September.

1. What are some of your Musical Goals? What pieces would you like to finish? How about popular music? What about your own compositions? What about performances with another family member? More ideas . . .

Goals from last term	*Goals for this term*

2. Take a look at the following Life Skills: empathy, humor, persistence, accuracy, excellence, reflection, communication, creativity, independence, precision, taking risks, get organized, cooperate. More ideas . . .

Identify your current Life Skills	*Identify Life Skills to work on*

3. Your Own Musical Project. Brainstorm topics or themes for presentations.

Thanks so much,

Dr. Thompson

Appendix C

Everyday Musical Connections Projects

Please feel free to copy and paste the following templates for everyday musical connections (EMC) projects.

1. Tell Your Musical Story: I use this activity with junior high and senior high school students to get them thinking more purposely about their own musical background. It makes a great introduction to the EMC project.
2. Everyday Musical Connections Project: I use this template to help students zero in on a topic for exploration. Please note that students may take their inspiration in various directions:
   - Information projects: Numbers 1–4
   - Storytelling project: Number 5. Students may have a story they want to tell.
   - Teaching project: Number 6. Students may want to share their insight in teaching a musical aspect.
3. Project Preparation: During students' weekly lesson, I use this template to guide our discussions.
4. Presentation Checklist: I use this template the week before presentations are made. It's especially helpful in guiding information projects and storytelling projects.
5. EMC Project Evaluation: I use this template during the lesson period following students' presentation to provide my own feedback.
6. Follow-up Questionnaire: I use this template to allow students to reflect on their projects. Question 4 is valuable in deciding whether or not to continue exploring the current topic or to move on to another idea.

Appendix C

TELL YOUR MUSICAL STORY

Every student has their own musical story to tell. It consists of the many ways in which music occurs in a person's life. It includes those events, places, times, and people when music was there at times in full force and at other times hidden away in the background. To put together your own musical story, you may want to incorporate some of the following ideas:

1. What's the first piece of music you remember hearing? What was going on at the time? Who was involved?
2. What's the first piece of music you remember playing or singing? How did you feel at that time?
3. The following words describe how a person may feel about music. Choose as many words as you want and tell why you include these words. Music may be your companion, distraction, escape, entertainment, friend, inspiration, reminder, background, energy, refuge, catalyst, mood, physical, emotional, flow, energy, movement, spirit.
4. What words would you add to the above list? Describe why those words are important to how you feel about music?
5. How has the music in your life been influenced by your parents, family members, and friends? In what ways? How do you feel about it?
6. Musical events or concerts can be both formal and completely unexpected. What musical events or concerts are part of your story? Where did they take place? Who was involved?
7. What other questions or aspects of your own choice would you like to include?

Appendix C

Everyday Musical Connections Project

Music shows up in every person's life in an endless number of unique and interesting everyday musical connections. Over the coming weeks, your task will be to explore or investigate a topic inspired by your everyday musical connections. You will present your results in the form of a video or keynote presentation in group class and in a public presentation. To get started, have a look at the following suggestions for topics.

1. What musical topic would you like to know more about? Choose three aspects of music that intrigue you:
   a. _____
   b. _____
   c. _____

2. Musical comparisons may provide you with an interesting topic. Look for similarities and differences when you compare
   a. two artists from the same genre
   b. two musical selections from a movie, your playlist
   c. two compositions with the same name

3. How does music show up in your daily life? Document a typical day. Provide an analysis. _____

4. What is something about music that bothers you? Why is this so?
   _____
   _____
   _____

5. Storytelling: Music often is valued for its story-telling value. You may have an entertaining story that involves music.
   _____
   _____
   _____

6. Teaching: There are many aspects of music that involve teaching. What musical aspect would you like to teach others about?
   _____
   _____
   _____

Format and Limits
- 3–4 minute oral presentation or video
- Maximum of 20 keynote slides

Presentation Dates
- Cycle 1 – Group Class presentation on _____
- Cycle 2 – Public presentation on _____

Project Preparation
Exploring Everyday Musical Connections

Use the following four stages to guide your process:

Create	Evaluate
• I'm exploring my interests & passions • I'm using knowledge & imagination	• I'm adapting my plan as I proceed • I'm watching for what works and what doesn't work

Everyday Musical Connections are the central focus

Investigate	Incorporate
• I'm experimenting with different possibilities • I'm finding people & resources that help	• I'm making sure others will understand my project • I'm making sure my project will be done on time

Presentation Checklist
Exploring Everyday Musical Connections

Information Presentation Essentials

Good presentations include: ✓ Good title ✓ Introduction or hook line ✓ Main points ✓ Supporting info ✓ Conclusions or summary ✓ Audience feedback	Good presenters: ✓ Introduce themselves ✓ Connect with the audience ✓ Talk loud enough ✓ Smile & make eye contact ✓ Look at the audience, not their slides or cue cards
Poster presentations ✓ 3-4 posters provide structure for the presentation	Keynote presentations ✓ Slides of engaging images ✓ Slides with bullet-point info

Everyday Musical Connections are the central focus

Storytelling Essentials

Good stories include: ✓ Good title ✓ Characters ✓ Setting, plot ✓ Conflict ✓ Resolution	Good storytellers: ✓ Introduce themselves ✓ Evoke emotions ✓ Share information ✓ Entertain ✓ Ask for audience feedback

Appendix C

EMC Project Evaluation				
Name:	**Date:**			
	High	Med.	Low	N/A
Everyday Musical Connection featured				
Presentation				
Good title				
Introduction or hook line				
Main points				
Supporting info				
Conclusions or summary				
Audience feedback				
Presenter				
Introduce themselves				
Connect with the audience				
Talk loud enough				
Smile & make eye contact				
Look at the audience				
Poster quality				
Slide quality				
Storytelling				
Good title				
Characters				
Setting, plot				
Conflict				
Resolution				
Story Presenter				
Introduce themselves				
Evoke emotions				
Share information				
Entertain				
Ask for audience feedback				

Appendix C

Follow-Up Questionnaire

Name:

Date:

Now that you've completed your project presentation, take some time to reflect on what you've achieved, how you got there, and what might happen next. Please respond thoughtfully to the following questions.

1. What did you learn about *yourself* through your music project?

   _____
   _____
   _____

2. What did you learn about *music?*

   _____
   _____
   _____

3. List five skills you used to put your presentation together.

   _____
   _____
   _____

4. What would you like to do next? Continue to refine your current project? Start a new project? What will you do differently?

   _____
   _____
   _____

Appendix D
Character Cards

I printed the following 2- by 4.25-inch cards and keep them scattered on the top of my piano for easy access.

Accuracy	Artistry	Authenticity
Beauty	Care	Challenge
Concentration	Cooperation	Creativity
Empathy	Excellence	Flexibility
Gratitude	Heart & Soul	Imagination
Independence	Kindness	Listen
Musicianship	Organize	Persistence
Refine	Reflection	Stick With It
Take Risks	Think First	

Bibliography

Allsup, Randall. 2002. "Mutual Learning and Democratic Action in Instrumental Music Education." *Journal of Research in Music Education* 51 (1): 24–37.
———. 2016. *Remixing the Classroom*. Bloomington: Indiana University Press.
Barenboim, D. 2008. *Everything Is Connected*. London, UK: Weldenfeld & Nicolson.
Bell, M., R. Fitzgerald, and M. Legge. 2013. "Parent Peer Advocacy, Information and Refusing Disability Discourses." *New Zealand Journal of Social Sciences Online* 8 (1–2): 1–12.
Benedict, C., P. Schmidt, G. Spruce, and P. Woodford. 2015. *The Oxford Handbook of Social Justice in Music Education*. New York: Oxford University Press.
Berk, R. A. 2003. *Professors Are From Mars and Students Are From Snickers*. Sterling, VI: Stylus.
Berlyne, D. E. 1954. "A Theory of Human Curiosity." *British Journal of Psychology* 45 (3): 180–91.
Bloom, B. 1985. *Developing Talent in Young People*. New York: Ballantine Books.
Boer, D. and A. Abubakar. 2014. "Music Listening in Families and Peer Groups: Benefits for Young People's Social Cohesion and Emotional Well-being Across Four Cultures." *Frontiers in Psychology* 5: 392. doi: 10.3389/fpsyg.2014.00392.
Brookfield, S. D. 2006. *The Skillful Teacher*. San Francisco, CA: Jossey-Boss.
Brown, P. C., H. L. Roediger, and M. A. McDaniel. 2014. *Make It Stick: The Science of Successful Learning*. Cambridge, MA: Harvard University Press.
Cain, Susan. 2013. *Quiet*. New York: Broadway Books.
Canter, L. and M. Canter. 1997. *Lee Canter's Assertive Discipline: Positive Behaviour Management for Today's Classroom*. Santa Monica, CA: Lee Canter and Associates.
Carey, Benedict. 2015. *How We Learn: The Surprising Truth about When, Where, and Why It Happens*. New York: Random House.
Collins, Anita. 2021. *The Music Advantage: How Music Helps Your Child Develop, Learn, and Thrive*. New York: TarcherPerigree.

Coloroso, Barbara. 1995. *Kids Are Worth It: Giving Your Child the Gift of Inner Discipline*. Toronto, ON: Somerville House Publishing.

Corkille Briggs, Dorothy. 1975. *Your Child's Self-esteem: The Key to Life*. Garden City, NY: Doubleday & Company.

Costa, A. L. and B. Kallick. 2008. *Learning and Leading with Habits of Mind*. Alexandria, VA: ASCD.

Covey, S. 1989. *The Seven Habits of Highly Effective People: Restoring the Character Ethic*. New York: Free Press.

Cox, D. G. and K. S. Meaney. 2018. "Lights, Camera, Project-based Learning!" *Strategies* 31 (11): 23–29.

Creech, A. 2009. "The Role of the Family in Supporting Learning." In *The Oxford Handbook of Music Psychology*, edited by S. Hallam and I. T. Cross, 295–306, Oxford, UK: Oxford University Press.

Cutietta, R. 2013. *Raising Musical Kids: A Guide for Parents*. Oxford, UK: Oxford University Press.

Daniel, R. and K. Parkes. 2015. "Assessment and Critical Feedback in the Master-Apprentice Relationship." In *Assessment in Music Education*, edited by D. Lebler, G. Carey, and S. Harrison, 107–24. New York: Springer.

Davidson, J., M. Howe, and J. Sloboda. 1995. "The Role of Parents in the Success and Failure of Instrumental Learner," *Bulletin of the Council for Research in Music Education* 127 (1995): 40–44.

Deci, E. and R. Ryan. 2002. *Handbook of Self-determination Research*. Rochester, NY: University of Rochester Press.

Demenga, Thomas. 2014. "The Art of Distraction is More Effective than Repetitive Practice." February 13, 2014. http://www.thestrad.com/the-art-of-distraction-is-more-effective-than-repetitive-practice/.

Dewey, H. 1933. *How We Think*. Boston, MA: Houghton Mifflin.

Ericsson, K. A., R. Krampe, and C. Tesch-Römer. 1993. "The Role of Deliberate Practice in the Acquisition of Expert Performance." *Psychological Review* 100 (3): 363–406.

Festinger, L. 1957. *A Theory of Cognitive Dissonance*. Stanford, CA: Stanford University Press.

Garner, R. 2006. "Humour in Pedagogy: How Ha-ha can Lead to Aha." *College Teaching* 54 (1): 177–180.

Gaunt, H. 2010. "One-to-one Tuition in a Conservatoire: The Perceptions of Instrumental and Vocal Students." *Psychology of Music* 38 (2): 178–208.

Gay, G. 2002. "Preparing for Culturally Responsive Teaching." *Journal of Teacher Education* 53 (106): 106–16.

Gonzalez-DeHass, A., P. Willems, and M. Doan Holbein. 2005. "Examining the Relationship Between Parental Involvement and Student Motivation." *Educational Psychology Review* 17: 99–123.

Grant, A. 2021. *Think Again*. New York: Viking.

Green, Lucy. 2002. *How Popular Musicians Learn*. Burlington, VT: Ashgate Publishing.

Groen, J. and C. Kawalilak. 2014. *Pathways of Adult Learning*. Toronto, ON: Canadian Scholars' Press.

Hammond, Wayne. 2003. "Understanding the Resiliency Framework." Resiliency Initiatives. Accessed May 1, 2021, https://shed-the-light.webs.com/documents/Understanding%20the%20Resiliency%20Framework.pdf.

Hammond, Zaretta. 2015. *Culturally Responsive Teaching and the Brain: Promoting Authentic Engagement and Rigor Among Culturally and Linguistically Diverse Students*. Thousand Oaks, CA: Corwin Press.

Hattie, John and Helen Timperley. 2007. "The Power of Feedback." *Review of Educational Research* 77 (1): 81–112.

Hendricks, Karin S. 2018. *Compassionate Music Teaching*. London: Rowman & Littlefield.

Hillman, James. 2017. *The Soul's Code*. New York: Ballantine Books.

Horvath, Janet. 2010. *Playing (Less) Hurt: An Injury Prevention Guide for Musicians*. Milwaukee, WI: Hal Leonard Books.

Hunter, J. D. 2001. *The Death of Character: Moral Education in an Age Without Good or Evil*. New York: Basic Books.

Huntley, H. E. 1970. *The Divine Proportion*. New York: Dover Publications.

Iscoe, L. and K. Bordelon. 1985. "Pilot Parents: Peer Support for Parents of Handicapped Children." *Children's Health Care* 14 (2): 103–9.

Jensen, Eric. 1995. *Super Teaching*, third edition. San Diego, CA: The Brain Store.

———. 2009. *Super Teaching*, fourth edition. Thousand Oaks, CA: Corwin Press.

Kilpatrick, W. H. 1918. "The Project Method." *Teachers College Record*, 19 (4): 319–335.

Kleinman, J. and P. Buckoke. 2013. *The Alexander Technique for Musicians*. London: Bloomsbury.

Ladson-Billings, G. 1995. "Toward a Theory of Culturally Relevant Pedagogy." *American Education Research Journal* 32 (3): 465–91.

Latukefu, L. and L. Verenikina. 2018. "Expanding the Master-Apprentice Model." In *Collaborative Learning in Higher Education*, edited by H. Gaunt and H. Westerlund, 101–9. Surrey, UK: Ashgate Publishing.

Larmer, J. and J. Mergendoller. 2010. "Seven Essentials for Project-based Learning." *Educational Leadership* 68 (2): 34–37.

Larmer, J., J. Mergendoller, and S. Boss. 2015. *Gold standard PBL: Essential project design elements*. Novato, CA: Buck Institute for Education.

Lind, V. R. and C. McKoy. 2016. *Culturally Responsive Teaching in Music Education*. New York: Taylor and Francis.

Luff, P., and D. Lebler. 2018. "Striking a Balance in Brass Pedagogy." In *Collaborative Learning in Higher Education*, edited by H. Gaunt and H. Westerlund, 173–77. Surrey, UK: Ashgate Publishing.

Mark, Thomas. 2003. *What Every Pianist Needs to Know about the Body*. Chicago: GIA Publications.

Markham, Thom. 2011. "Project Based Learning: A Bridge Just Far Enough." *Teacher Librarian* 39 (2): 38–42.

McPherson, G., and J. Davidson. 2006. "Playing an Instrument." In *The Child as Musician*, edited by G. McPherson, 331–51. Oxford, UK: Oxford University Press.

McPherson, G. E., J. W. Davidson, and R. Faulkner. 2012. *Music in Our Lives*. Oxford, UK: Oxford University Press.

Morioka, M. 1991. "The Concept of 'Inochi': A Philosophical Perspective on the Study of Life." *Japan Review* 2: 83–115.

Morrison, M. K. 2010. *Using Humor to Maximize Learning: The Links Between Positive Emotions and Education*. Plymouth, UK: Rowman & Littlefield Education.

Montessori, M. 1995. *The Absorbent Mind*. New York: Henry Holt.

Muhammad, Gholdy. 2020. *Cultivating Genius: An Equity Framework for Culturally and Historically Responsive Literacy*. New York: Scholastic.

Nathan, A. 2014. *The Music Parents' Survival Guide: A Parent-to-parent Conversation*. Oxford: Oxford University Press.

Noddings, Nel. 2005. *The Challenge to Care in Schools: An Alternative Approach to Education,* New York: Teachers College Press.

Phillippen, P. B. 2012. "The Effects of Smiling and Frowning on Perceived Affect and Exertion While Physically Active." *Journal of Sport Behavior* 35 (3): 337–53.

Pink, Daniel. 2009. *Drive: The Surprising Truth about What Motivates Us*. New York: Riverhead Books.

Pollei, Paul. 1991. "Our Evolving Profession." *The Piano Quarterly* 39 (153): 54–55.

Popov, L. K., D. Popov, and D. Kavelin. "The Virtues Project." https://virtuesproject.com.

Rogers, C. and H. J. Freiberg. 1994. *Freedom to Learn*, third edition. New York: Macmillan College Publishing.

Ross, Alex. 2020. "The Fearless Pianist." *The New Yorker*, May 18, 2020.

Rowe, Mary Budd. 1986. "Wait Time: Slowing Down May Be a Way of Speeding Up!" *Journal of Teacher Education* 37 (1): 43–50.

Rudney, G. L. 2005. *Every Teacher's Guide to Working with Parents*. Thousand Oaks, CA: Corwin Press.

Sartwell, C. 2004. *Six Names of Beauty*. London: Routledge.

Seligman, Martin E. P. 2011. *Flourish: A Visionary New Understanding of Happiness and Well-being*. New York: Atria.

Shearer, Carrie. 2020. "The Cultural Implications of Silence Around the World," accessed May 1, 2021, https://www.rw-3.com/blog/cultural-implications-of-silence.

Subramaniam, P. R. 2010. "Unlocking the Power of Situational Interest in Physical Education." *Journal of Physical Education, Recreation, & Dance*, 81 (7): 38–49.

Sussman, Warren. 2012. *Culture as History: The Transformation of American Society*. New York: Random House.

Suzuki, Shinichi. 1969. *Nurtured by Love*. Hicksville, NY: Exposition Press.

Swinkin, Jeffrey. 2015. *Teaching Performance: A Philosophy of Piano Pedagogy*. Dordrecht, Netherlands: Springer Publications.

Taylor, C. 1991. *The Ethics of Authenticity*. Cambridge, MA: Harvard University Press.

Taylor, Nancy. 2016. *Teaching Healthy Musicianship: The Music Educator's Guide to Injury Prevention and Wellness*. New York: Oxford University Press.

Thompson, Julia. 1998. *Discipline Survival Kit for the Secondary Teacher.* West Nyack, NY: The Center for Applied Research in Education.
Warren, A. M. 2016. *Project-based Learning Across the Disciplines.* Thousand Oaks, CA: Corwin.
Wasserman, Selma. 1992. *Asking the Right Question: The Essence of Teaching.* Bloomington, IN: Phi Beta Kappa Educational Foundation.
Westney, W. 2003. *The Perfect Wrong Note.* Pompton Plains, NJ: Amadeus Press.
Wolk, S. 1994. "Project-based Learning: Pursuits with a Purpose." *Educational Leadership* 52 (3): 42–45.
Ziegler, A. and M. M. Johns. 2012. "Health Promotion and Injury Education for Student Singers." *Journal of Singing* 68 (5): 531–41.

Index

accept–able tension, 36–38
accumulated repertoire. *See* review and refinement
artistry, *see* musicianship
authenticity, 8, 16, 91, 93, 99, 114–15, 144, 160–63, 165–66, 170, 178, 182
autonomy, 15, 49, 53–67, 74, 177;
    assumptions about, 55–56
    in the first lesson, 65
    synchronize teaching with students', 64–65
    teachers' belief in, 63
    See also independence
awareness, 119–22, 133

basic human needs, 49–51
beauty, 93–94, 99

caring, 8, 11, 102, 104, 113–14, 181–82;
    for music, 95–96
challenges, 76–79, 185–88
character, 15, 157–79;
    cards, 166–67, 179, 201
    etymological roots, 160
    exercises, 170–76, 179
    historical differentiation, 160
commitment to music lessons, 42–43
competency. *See* fluency
concerts, 64–65, 82, 86–87, 135–36
creativity, 76–79
culturally responsive teaching, 6–8, 19

curriculum models, 3–6

deliberate practice, 74–75
demonstration and explanation, 66, 117, 119–21, 167
diversity. *See* culturally responsive teaching

efficiency in teaching, 31, 57, 58, 59
empathy, 8, 113–14, 145, 164, 171–72, 177–78, 182
everyday musical connections, 141–42

family home life, 14–16
fluency, 50, 69–88, 177;
    immersion in activity, 71–73
follow-up, 81, 126

harmful practice strategies, 60–62
homework notes, 29–32, 62–63;
    student engagement, 31
human needs. *See* basic human needs
humor, 110–13

inclusion. *See* culturally responsive teaching
independence, 16, 19–22
injury prevention. *See* harmful practice strategies
inochi, 96–97

junior high threshold, 151–52

language, 56–59, 78, 92–92, 99;
   and gestures, 20–22, 56–59, 106
learning processes, 34–35, 78
letter, parent, 189–90;
   teenager, 191
Levit, Igor, 176–77
life skills, 164–68
listening, 50, 133–37

mastery. *See* fluency
mistakes, 21, 59–60
musicianship, 90–93, 99

National Association for Music Education, 169–70
non-performance projects. *See* projects

100 Days Practice Club, 84–85
ownership, 66;
   See also independence, autonomy

parents, 13–44;
   check-ins, 128–29, 131
   diverse needs, 28–29
   evolving participation, 26–28
   most practical resource, 38–40
   opening doors for, 42
   questions, 33–36
peers, parents, 38–40;
   students, 136
playfulness, 43–44
popular musicians, 55
positive mindset, 85–86
practicing,
   for concert performance, 86–87
   not practicing, 87
   slow practice, 82–84
project-based learning, 142–45;
   teacher's role in, 145–46
projects, 141–56;
   templates, 193–200
purpose, 50, 89–100, 177

questions, 122–24, 130

RCM exams, 3
reflection, 50, 72, 117–32, 144–45, 155, 174–75, 178;
   written reflections, 99, 167
relatedness, 19, 25–27, 50, 56, 101–16, 177
repetition, 73–75, 77–79
report cards, 126–28, 130–31
respect, 18–19
review and refinement, 79–82

self-determination theory, 50
sense of humor. *See* humor
shared curriculum, 3–5;
   50/50 approach, 64
silence, 124–25;
   in different cultures, 7
slow practice, 82–84
smiling, 108–10
soul, exercises, 173
spirituality, 97, 99, 141
stories, 98, 153–54
student-centered teaching, 1–2
student-led curriculum, 3–5
student-sensitive curriculum 3–5
switching teachers, 40–41
Suzuki, Shinichi, 96–97, 169
   method, 3, 169–70

teacher-led curriculum, 3–5
teen student reviews, 129–30
"Tiger Mom" actions, 38
trust, 42–43, 56
uncomfortable circumstances, 40–41

varied practice, 78, 81, 85
vision of life, 96–97, 99

words and actions. *See* language and gestures

About the Author

Merlin B. Thompson (PhD, MA, BMus) is an award-winning music educator, scholar, and pianist with more than four decades of music studio teaching experience. He has worked with hundreds of music teachers, students, and parents in workshops, conferences, established programs, and mentorships in online formats and in-person throughout Canada, the United States, Australia, Japan, Spain, Great Britain, Brazil, and New Zealand. He is a frequent consultant, advisor, and mentor for music studio teachers around the world. A graduate of the Talent Education Institute in Matsumoto, Japan, Merlin is a forward-thinking Suzuki piano teacher trainer. His recent academic teaching experiences include music pedagogy for undergraduate students in the Schulich School of Music at McGill University and professional development and a social justice approach to K–12 diversity for B.Ed students in the Werklund School of Education at the University of Calgary. He is the creator and producer of the podcast series: *The Music Educator's Crucible*. His video series *Fundamental Piano Technique* is available on YouTube.

Made in the USA
Middletown, DE
08 April 2022